The Andersonville Trial is Saul Levitt's first play. A shorter version was presented on television in 1957.

Saul Levitt was born in Hartford, Connecticut, but he has been a New Yorker since the age of three, and is a graduate of New York's City College. During World War II he was a radio operator on a B-17, and then Staff Representative for the Army magazine *Yank*, attached to the Third Army.

Mr. Levitt has written a novel, *The Sun Is Silent*, and short stories which have appeared in *Cosmopolitan*, *American Mercury* and *Harper's* magazine. He has written extensively for television and documentary films.

THE ANDERSONVILLE TRIAL

Random House, New York

A play by Saul Levitt

THE ANDERSONVILLE TRIAL

Photographs by courtesy of Friedman-Abeles

Library of Congress Catalog Card Number: 60–12143

Manufactured in the United States of America

For Dena

The basic source material for this play is the official record of the actual trial of Henry Wirz, which took place in Washington, D.C. in the summer of 1865. The play may be considered "documentary" to the following extent: that it is set in the time and place circumstance of the historical trial; that the formal roles and names of its characters repeat those of the historical participants; and that some of the dialogue derives from the trial record. It might be added that the theme expressed in the play inheres in the trial record. Essentially, however, the play expresses the author's own conception of the personalities and the occasion—and is to be read as "drama" and not as "documentary."

THE ANDERSONVILLE TRIAL *was first presented by William Darrid, Eleanore Saidenberg, and Daniel Hollywood at Henry Miller's Theatre, New York City, on December 29, 1959, with the following cast:*

(IN ORDER OF SPEAKING)

GENERAL LEW WALLACE	Russell Hardie
PRESIDENT OF THE COURT	
LIEUTENANT	Robert Burr
COURT CLERK	Heywood Hale Broun
LT. COL. N. P. CHIPMAN	George C. Scott
THE JUDGE ADVOCATE	
OTIS H. BAKER	Albert Dekker
THE DEFENSE COUNSEL	
CAPTAIN WILLIAMS	Al Henderson
HENRY WIRZ	Herbert Berghof
THE DEFENDANT	
LIEUTENANT COLONEL CHANDLER	Robert Carroll
LOUIS SCHADE	James Arenton
ASSISTANT DEFENSE COUNSEL	
DR. JOHN C. BATES	Ian Keith
AMBROSE SPENCER	Moultrie Patten
DR. C. M. FORD	Douglas Herrick
PRISON SURGEON	
JAMES H. DAVIDSON	James Greene
MAJOR D. HOSMER	Howard Wierum
ASSISTANT JUDGE ADVOCATE	

JASPER CULVER	Robert Gerringer
GEORGE W. GRAY	Frank Sutton
UNION SOLDIERS	Robert Downey, Martin West, Lou Frizzell
COURT REPORTER	Vincent Donahue
NEWSPAPERMEN	Robert Mayer, Richard Poston, William Scharf

GENERAL MOTT
GENERAL THOMAS
GENERAL GEARY
GENERAL FESSENDEN ⎬ ASSISTING JUDGES ⎨ Clifford Carpenter
GENERAL BALLIER Taylor Graves
COLONEL ALLCOCK John Leslie
COLONEL STIBBS Owen Pavitt
William Hussung
Archie Smith
Freeman Meskimen

Directed by JOSÉ FERRER

Production designed and lighted by WILL STEVEN ARMSTRONG

ACT ONE

SCENE ONE

The Court of Claims, Washington, D.C. A morning in August, 1865. The atmosphere is sweltering.

The set reflects the musty courtroom of the historical trial—a room framed by heavy columns rising to form high arches which support a vaulted ceiling. A chandelier is suspended above the JUDGES' table. A number of conference-type tables are arranged to form a courtroom area: defense and prosecution tables, right and left, are on opposite sides; the JUDGES' table is center and to the rear, so that the JUDGES will sit facing the audience; the witness chair is placed near the JUDGES' table. Next to the defense table we note the bizarre element of a chaise longue. It is for the prisoner, who is ill and who will recline through most of the trial. Two tall French windows take up a large part of one wall. Set in the opposite wall are the double doors which form the only entrance into the room. A bench has been placed near the windows, with a railing in front of it which separates it from the courtroom area. It will serve as the "press gallery." Set close to the railing is a small table for the use of both the COURT CLERK and the COURT REPORTER. An American flag is mounted on the wall behind the JUDGES' table. On a stand, behind the JUDGES' table, is a huge schematic drawing of the Andersonville stockade —a rectangle with a simple sketching in of elements such as a stream, walls, entrance gate, "deadline," "hospital," burial ground, etc.

At rise: all parties to the trial, with the exception of the JUDGES and the defendant, are present. Only the three newspapermen and the two defense lawyers wear civilian clothes. The others

3

wear the blue uniforms of the Union Army. The military trial will begin in a moment, but in the meanwhile people stand and sit and converse in small groups. The two soldiers standing guard at the open doors slouch negligently. The atmosphere as the play opens is casual.

The JUDGE ADVOCATE *and* ASSISTANT JUDGE ADVOCATE *are* LIEUTENANT COLONEL N. P. CHIPMAN *and* MAJOR D. HOSMER. *Opposite them are* OTIS H. BAKER *and* LOUIS SCHADE, *representing the defendant.*

Now CAPTAIN WILLIAMS *enters, moving to the* LIEUTENANT *in charge of the courtroom guard detail, to whom he whispers with an air of suppressed excitement. (As we will learn in a moment, the exchange refers to the absence of the defendant). The* LIEUTENANT *imparts his information to* CHIPMAN *and starts in the direction of* BAKER, *then at a signal from one of the soldiers he goes swiftly toward the doors. He halts near them to stand stiffly, shouting, "Attention!" All parties come to attention as the* JUDGES, *eight Union officers of rank, take their places. They sit, flanking* GENERAL LEW WALLACE, *President of the Court. There is a quality of cold, overriding power and purpose in control as proceedings start.*

As WALLACE *speaks, he reveals a chill and remote authority. He is a major general, thirty-seven years of age.*

WALLACE (*Banging gavel down once*)   This military court convened by order of the War Department is now in session. The Lieutenant in charge is advised to post additional guards in the corridor. A lane must be kept clear at all times to the courtroom doors.

LIEUTENANT   Yes, sir.
  (*He goes out*)

4

WALLACE   Have all witnesses listed to appear in these proceedings reported to the Clerk of the Court?

CLERK   All have reported to the Clerk, sir, and are on hand.

WALLACE   I take it all concerned with these proceedings have signed the necessary oath of allegiance to the government of the United States.

CLERK   Yes, sir.
   (*The* LIEUTENANT *re-enters and takes up his post at the closed doors*)

WALLACE   (*As he refers to counsel by name, they acknowledge their names by a nod*)   Lieutenant Colonel N. P. Chipman, for the War Department. Mr. Otis Baker for the defense. The defendant, Henry Wirz, is to be tried by this military commission consisting of—(*Glancing down the line of the* JUDGES) General Mott . . . General Thomas . . . General Geary . . . General Fessenden . . . General Ballier . . . Colonel Allcock . . . Colonel Stibbs . . . and myself, General Wallace. Has the defense any objection to any of its members?

BAKER   No objection.

WALLACE   I do not see the defendant.

CHIPMAN   If the Court please, Captain Williams is here and will explain his absence.
   (CAPTAIN WILLIAMS *comes forward*)

WILLIAMS   Sir, regarding the defendant. He will be brought here shortly.

WALLACE   Is he ill?

WILLIAMS (*Blurting it*)   Sir, he is temporarily indisposed, following his attempt on his life early this morning which was foiled by the alertness of the guards—

WALLACE   Mr. Wirz attempted to take his life?

WILLIAMS   Unsuccessfully, sir.

WALLACE   Captain, you will explain to the Court how such an attempt could have possibly occurred.

WILLIAMS   Sir, Mr. Wirz tried to slash his wrist after breaking a bottle.

WALLACE   A bottle?

WILLIAMS   A brandy bottle which he receives daily as a stimulant by order of Dr. Ford—

WALLACE   The incident should not have occurred— You are charged with custody of the prisoner. You will take the necessary steps so it will not occur again. You say the prisoner is in condition to appear shortly?

WILLIAMS   Within a few minutes, and I will personally—

WALLACE (*Cutting him off*)   That is all.

WILLIAMS   Yes, sir.
          (*He exits, to re-enter later with* CAPTAIN WIRZ)

WALLACE   I will ask defense counsel to plead to the indictment in the absence of the defendant.

BAKER   We would prefer, if the Court will permit, that Captain Wirz hear the charges against him directly—

WALLACE   This trial has been postponed several times and the Court intends to proceed this morning without further delay. (*More a command than a question*) Will counsel plead to the charge?

BAKER   Counsel will plead.

WALLACE   If the Judge Advocate is ready.

CHIPMAN   Ready, sir.

WALLACE   The indictment will be read.

(CHIPMAN's *movement reflects something of the man at once. He is thirty-one, a battle veteran whose youthful idealism has been hardened by war to a fierce unyielding partisanship. We must sense humane impulses held underneath a compulsion of bitterness toward the South— warring feelings creating a quality of controlled tension*)

CHIPMAN   Charge— Criminal conspiracy to destroy the lives of soldiers of the United States in violation of the laws and customs of war.

Specification— That Henry Wirz who was in charge of the Confederate Prison at Andersonville, Georgia, did keep in barbarously close confinement federal soldiers, up to the number of forty thousand, without adequate shelter against the burning heat of summer or the cold of winter and—

7

Specification— That the said Henry Wirz in carrying out this conspiracy did not provide the prisoners of war with sufficient food, clothing or medical care, causing them to languish and die to the number of more than fourteen thousand.

Specification— That he established a line known as the "deadline" and that he instructed the prison guards stationed on the walls of the prison stockade to fire upon and kill any prisoner who might pass beyond that deadline.

Specification— That he used bloodhounds to hunt down, seize and mangle escaping prisoners of war, through these various causes bringing about the deaths of about fifty federal soldiers, their names unknown.

Specification— That through direct order and/or by his own hand he brought about the murder of thirteen prisoners, their names unknown.

WALLACE   Mr. Baker, pleading for the prisoner—how do you plead to the charge?

BAKER   (*He is in his forties; a lawyer of polish, experience, and daring; of an ironic, worldly intelligence. Method must be sensed in his every move—even when he appears most angry. We hear the edge of irony in his voice as he makes his objections; aware that they are all going to be rejected*)   We interpose a motion—that this military Court discharge itself as being without proper jurisdiction now that the war is over.

CHIPMAN   This Court has jurisdiction under the war powers of the President, which are still in force. It is well known that die-hard Rebel officers still refuse to lay down their arms. Officially and in fact the war continues. Move to deny.

8

WALLACE The motion is denied.

BAKER Motion to postpone . . . on the ground that potential witnesses who in more normal times might speak for the defendant refuse to do so now, for fear their motives will be misunderstood as signifying support of the late Confederacy.

CHIPMAN (*With open sarcasm*) If Mr. Baker's witnesses can in good conscience take the oath of loyalty to the government of the United States, they have nothing to fear.

BAKER The Court is aware of the temper of the times. It is only four short months since Mr. Lincoln was assassinated.

WALLACE (*A clap of thunder*) We will leave that name out of this trial!

BAKER Nevertheless, Mr. Lincoln's presence is in this room—his murder is felt in this room—and it swells the charge of murder against the defendant to gigantic size—

CHIPMAN For which the Southern cause is responsible. And counsel will not turn Mr. Lincoln's tragic death to his advantage here.

BAKER It is my general concern, sir, that the indictment leaves out Captain Wirz's military superiors, making him the single target of the national mood of vengeance against the South—

WALLACE (*Gavel*) That will be all, Mr. Baker. Motion denied. If you have no further motions—

BAKER I do. As to the specifications alleging the crime of murder and abetting murder against certain persons, move to strike them since no persons are named.

CHIPMAN Counsel cannot with his motions dispose of the horror of fourteen thousand unknown dead dumped into unmarked graves at Andersonville. Better records were kept of bales of cotton. Move to deny.

BAKER Will the Judge Advocate tell us where accurate prison records were kept during the war? (CHIPMAN *reacts with obvious annoyance*) The Judge Advocate owes me common courtesy here. He forgets that a person accused of crimes punishable by death is entitled to a proper defense.

CHIPMAN We know what is defended here. Counsel's political motives are well understood.

WALLACE (*Raps gavel*) The exchange will stop.

BAKER I only remind the Judge Advocate that he is in a court of law and no longer on the battlefield. He behaves as if the horror of war was not universal. The North had its Andersonvilles.

WALLACE The government of the United States is not on trial here, Mr. Baker.

BAKER That remains to be seen.

WALLACE (*Rising*) Mr. Baker—!

BAKER   Meaning no offense to the Court— The remark stated in full would have been . . . "That remains to be seen through the testimony that will be offered here." I was referring to what the record will show, sir . . .

WALLACE   The Court is not misled—(*The courtroom door is opened from the outside by* CAPTAIN WILLIAMS, *who indicates to the* LIEUTENANT *in charge that the prisoner is ready to appear*) In the future you will exercise care in your remarks to this court, Mr. Baker. Motion denied.

LIEUTENANT   Prisoner to the Court!
        (WIRZ *enters, followed by* DR. FORD, *who carries his medical bag and who is followed by* CAPTAIN WILLIAMS. FORD *and* WILLIAMS *go above witness chair to sit in reporters' area, in front of the windows. Dressed in shabby black clothes and a white shirt open at the throat, obviously not well,* WIRZ *still manages to suggest the bearing of a soldier. He looks about him as he moves toward the defense table— arrogant, defiant, fatalistic, contemptuous—a mixture of all these attitudes. He is in his forties*)

WALLACE   (*To* BAKER)   If you have no further motions, I will order the defendant to plead to the charge.

BAKER   No further motion, but if the Court please, we have made a special request of the Judge Advocate on behalf of the defendant—which he has apparently forgotten.

CHIPMAN   (*Cold*)   It has been requested that the prisoner be permitted to recline on a sofa during the proceedings on his claim of great pain and weakness owing to a so-called war wound—

WIRZ (*He speaks with a slight Germanic accent*) Not so-called, Colonel. I was a soldier in the line. I was honorably wounded at the Battle of Seven Pines, and—

CHIPMAN The defendant is not the only man in this room who bears the scars of war.

WIRZ I will not be slandered.

WALLACE Permission is granted for the prisoner to recline during the proceedings, and he will now plead—

WIRZ (*Breaking in swiftly; speaking with heavy irony; he is still standing*) I thank you, General. I wish to make a statement, sir, as to my—

WALLACE You will have an opportunity to do so—

WIRZ (*Finishing*) —as to my attempt on my own life this morning, if the Court is interested—

WALLACE Make your statement.

WIRZ It was not guilt of conscience that drove me to that act. I have no guilt of conscience. None whatsoever—

WALLACE If that is all you have to say—

WIRZ Only a few words more, sir. I calmly sized up the situation, as a soldier. As I see it I have simply no chance whatsoever and I decided not to give the government the satisfaction—

WALLACE (*Overlapping*) That will be all, Mr. Wirz.

WIRZ One other matter, sir—

WALLACE That will be all.

WIRZ Then the Court will not permit me to mention a personal matter that should be the concern of the Court?

WALLACE You will speak to the point—what is it?

WIRZ I write letters to my family and do not know if they are received.

WALLACE The Court has nothing to do with mails. Possibly your letters are delayed. Conditions are still unsettled.

WIRZ General, I was taken from the midst of my family without warning and under the eyes of my children arrested. I do not care what the newspapers call me—let them call me the butcher of Andersonville. But what my children think of their father—that is important to me. I have a right to present myself as I wish to my children. *I have that right.* It is a cruelty that I do not know if my letters are received.
      (*The* JUDGES *confer briefly*)

WALLACE If you wish, we will see to it that your letters go by military packet to your home—

WIRZ (*Appearing to fawn; but with irony*) I thank the Court most kindly. They have been most considerate to me. The medical care, the spiritual comfort of the priest who is permitted to visit me daily in my cell. The Court has been most kind. (*With sudden venom*) All that is wanted of me is my life. I am not fooled!

BAKER (*Crosses to* WIRZ *and escorts him to the couch as he addresses the Court*) Will the Court make due allowance for the strain the defendant is under—?

CHIPMAN (*Overlapping*) Defense counsel must share guilt with the prisoner for that outburst—
    (*As* CHIPMAN *and* BAKER *now quarrel,* WALLACE *remains stonily silent*)

BAKER (*Overlapping*) Everything is conspiracy in the eyes of the Judge Advocate— I'm not here to help you make your case —much as you would like—

CHIPMAN I would like you to be still now—

BAKER (*Overlapping*) And I remind you—that normal courtroom behavior—

CHIPMAN Nothing is normal here, sir—

BAKER —that normal courtroom behavior calls for the outward appearance—I don't care what you *think*—that one's opponent is acting in good faith—

CHIPMAN Which I cannot assume, sir, since I know where you stand—

BAKER And where is that, Colonel?

CHIPMAN On the side of those who secretly opposed this government when it was fighting for its life. Who pays you here?

BAKER Not the government.

CHIPMAN   No, not this government but the remnants of that other—still active.

BAKER   Make a political accusation against a man and nothing he says will be considered for its own sake. The Judge Advocate is suspicious of my politics and wants to know who pays me. (*Glancing toward* WALLACE) If the Court please, I'll oblige the Judge Advocate. (WALLACE *says nothing and* BAKER *moves to confront* CHIPMAN *at close range*) I am paid by a committee formed to defend Captain Wirz. I am not involved in this case in the way the Judge Advocate would wish. I take my cases where I find them, subject to one condition—I must feel there's a shade—the smallest shade of doubt—as to a man's guilt. (*As he strides back to the defense table*) Regarding my politics, in my home city of Baltimore, a city of divided loyalties, some held that I was an enemy to the Confederate side because I felt that slavery was not worth dying for since it was an unworkable institution that was doomed to extinction anyway. And there were the others who suspected me because I was lukewarm on the glorious future that would follow a Northern victory. The Colonel might make his own position clearer.

CHIPMAN   I will try to do that, Mr. Baker. I was brought up to believe that slavery was evil. I answered Mr. Lincoln's second call for volunteers because it was natural for me to go to war against a cause which wished to perpetuate human bondage. And I am here in the service of the Union to secure justice for men barbarously murdered by that Southern cause. I am personally involved here, Mr. Baker, if you are not—

BAKER   As a lawyer or as a clerk under orders to process Wirz through to the hangman? (CHIPMAN *comes to his feet, is re-*

strained by HOSMER, *sits.* BAKER *gestures toward* CHIPMAN *as he speaks to* SCHADE, *his voice cool*) As I thought. We can make the bull charge.

(WALLACE's *glance moves from* CHIPMAN *to* BAKER *in a long, silent chastising, after which he speaks in a flatly powerful tone*)

WALLACE I take it gentlemen are through . . . Under military law we could of course dispense with defense counsel; the defendant would not have to be present. And this case could be heard in a small room. But the government has seen fit to set it here in the Court of Claims and before an audience. Conceding the temper of the times and the emotions of all parties, we intend to hold this trial within bounds. I do not advise further testing the power of the Court to maintain order . . . (*Briskly*) Defense counsel has stated he has no further motions and I will now order the defendant to plead to the charge. Prisoner, how do you plead?

BAKER The prisoner enters a plea of not guilty to the charge and all specifications.

WALLACE The Judge Advocate will summon his first witness.
(*As* CHIPMAN *begins*, WIRZ *beckons to* BAKER)

CHIPMAN On the general charge of criminal conspiracy, we summon Mr. D. T. Chandler.
(*In the time it takes for* CHANDLER's *name to be bawled out by the* LIEUTENANT, *for* CHANDLER *to appear, walk to the witness chair, and be sworn, we hear the exchange at the defense table.* BAKER *tries to confer with* SCHADE, *but is interrupted by* WIRZ. *We must sense* BAKER's *quiet distaste for* WIRZ *as a person*)

WIRZ Baker, you have all the necessary documents—

LIEUTENANT (*Calls off*) Mr. D. T. Chandler!

BAKER Yes.

WIRZ And the evidence that I released the youngest Northern
prisoners on parole—you remember how I let them out to pick
blackberries—
(CHANDLER *enters and crosses to the* CLERK)

BAKER I know.
(CHANDLER *is sworn in by the* CLERK)

WIRZ (*Pause*) But it will do no good. (*The tone is cryptic*) I
must die . . . Yes . . . I must die . . . (*Pause*) The real
crime I have committed, Baker—you understand what it is of
course.

BAKER Well?

WIRZ That I chose the losing side.

CHIPMAN Before we begin we will state briefly the rule of evidence applying in cases of criminal conspiracy. The evidence
of a common design to commit a criminal act is sufficient to
convict—and we shall prove that such a common design ex-
isted at Andersonville—to which the defendant willingly lent
himself. (GENERAL WALLACE *indicates that* CHIPMAN *may start
interrogation. We should see* CHANDLER *as a man of breeding
and courage, caught through the questioning between loyalty
to his defeated cause and his essential humanity*) Mr. Chandler, please state how you were employed during the year 1864.

CHANDLER I served in the Army of the Confederacy, with the rank of lieutenant colonel.

CHIPMAN What was your official duty?

CHANDLER I was assigned by the war office to inspect and report on the military prisons maintained by the Confederacy.

CHIPMAN Did you, in the course of an official assignment, go to the Andersonville military prison situated in Sumter County, Georgia?

CHANDLER Yes, sir. There had been civilian complaints forwarded to Richmond.

CHIPMAN How long did you remain at Andersonville?

CHANDLER Two weeks.

CHIPMAN (*Moves to the map, indicating with a pointer*) I ask you if that is a fair map of the Andersonville stockade?

CHANDLER Yes, it is.

CHIPMAN Will you state the dimensions of the stockade—its area?

CHANDLER A thousand feet on the longer side, from north to south. Eight hundred feet from east to west, covering about sixteen acres of ground.

CHIPMAN (*Crosses to the prosecution table*) What was the nature of the terrain?

CHANDLER   Simply earth—bare ground.

CHIPMAN   Was that the condition of the terrain in advance of it being selected as a site for the camp?

CHANDLER   No, sir. The tract was originally part of a section of pine woods.

CHIPMAN   And what can you tell us of the climate in that part of Georgia? I refer now to extremes of temperature. Of summer heat and winter cold.

CHANDLER   In July and August it would be quite high, at times over a hundred degrees. Winters, it could be near freezing and rainy.

CHIPMAN   Was that camp laid out with provision for shelter of any kind?

CHANDLER   No, sir.

CHIPMAN   (*Moving to the map again, using the pointer*)   This outer stockade wall—describe it, sir.

CHANDLER   A wall some fifteen to twenty feet high, consisting of rough-hewn timbers. A platform ran along the top of the wall and at regular intervals there were sentry boxes.

CHIPMAN   This line inside the wall—

CHANDLER   That was a line of posts running parallel to the outer wall—about twenty-five feet inside it.

CHIPMAN It had a name, did it not?

CHANDLER The deadline—so called because a prisoner going beyond it could be shot by the guards.

CHIPMAN This meandering line?

CHANDLER That would be the stream that ran through the camp, entering under the wall on the west . . . and emerging under the east wall of the stockade.

CHIPMAN Its width and depth?

CHANDLER No more than a yard wide and perhaps a foot in depth . . . (*As* CHIPMAN *indicates with the pointer*) The marshy area around the stream.

CHIPMAN That marshy area could better be called swamp, could it not?

CHANDLER Yes, sir; swamp.

CHIPMAN Of what size?

CHANDLER Extending about a hundred and fifty feet on either side of the stream.

CHIPMAN And having a considerable oozy depth, did it not?

CHANDLER Anyone venturing across it would probably sink to his waist . . . (*Following the pointer*) That would be the cookhouse . . . The burial trenches . . . The deadhouse . . . The main-entrance gate—

CHIPMAN (*Crosses to his table*) Now, sir, as to the history of the camp. Will you state the circumstances under which it was established?

CHANDLER By the latter part of '63 our prisoner-of-war camps were overcrowded. The War Office then decided to create a new camp.

CHIPMAN Who was responsible for the establishment of this new camp?

CHANDLER General John H. Winder.

CHIPMAN Now deceased?

CHANDLER Yes.

CHIPMAN And what was his official function?

CHANDLER He was in charge of all military prisons for the Confederacy, east of the Mississippi.

CHIPMAN You have said the tract of land on which the camp was located was originally part of a section of pine woods. The cutting down of every tree that might have provided shade— was Winder responsible for that?

CHANDLER Yes, sir.

CHIPMAN And this site—and the arrangements made for the care of the prisoners was known to and approved by the War Office?

CHANDLER (*Tightly*) I cannot say how much knowledge or approval. The Colonel knows how a line of command operates.

CHIPMAN (*Moves to the witness*) Wasn't it their responsibility—? Withdrawn for the time being. Will you now describe conditions in the prison at Andersonville as you observed them?

CHANDLER The area was tightly crowded with men when I inspected it.

CHIPMAN Giving each prisoner—how much room, would you say?

CHANDLER Thirty-five-and-a-half square feet per prisoner.

CHIPMAN A space equivalent to a cell only six feet on each side. What else did you find at Andersonville?

CHANDLER (*Tightly*) There was a general insufficiency—of water, shelter, and food. I think that would cover it.

CHIPMAN (*Over the witness; his intensity is palpable*) I think not. When you say an insufficiency of water you mean that the available water supply for all purposes—for drinking, washing, cooking—all came from that narrow brook, is that correct?

CHANDLER Yes, sir.

CHIPMAN And that stream was at the same time the repository for all the waste matter at the camp, was it not?

22

CHANDLER Yes, sir.

CHIPMAN All waste was emptied into that stream; the waste from the cookhouse and the bodily waste of the prisoners?

CHANDLER Yes, sir.

CHIPMAN Making that stream into a foul, sluggish sink, isn't that so?

CHANDLER Yes—

CHIPMAN (*Circling*) And that foul, stinking stream a few feet wide was the water supply for forty thousand men, and that is what you meant by an insufficiency of water, isn't it?

CHANDLER Yes.

CHIPMAN And as to the insufficiency of shelter, there was in fact *no* shelter and the men lived on bare ground winter and summer or dug themselves into the ground, into burrows—is *that* correct?

CHANDLER Yes, sir.

CHIPMAN And as to the sort of clothing they had. You will please be specific, sir.

CHANDLER (*More and more uneasy*) *Some* wore shirts and trousers—

CHIPMAN *Some.* You mean the newly arrived prisoners *still* had their shirts and trousers, don't you?

23

CHANDLER Yes.

CHIPMAN You mean the rest, the vast number of them, were in rags, don't you?

CHANDLER Yes.

CHIPMAN You mean those men were simply in a state of nakedness and near nakedness under the terrible weather conditions you described a moment ago—isn't that so?

CHANDLER Yes.

CHIPMAN And the food?

CHANDLER Mostly corn meal.

CHIPMAN Ground fine or coarse?

CHANDLER Unbolted meal.

CHIPMAN Unbolted meal. Meaning meal ground so coarse it was as good as swallowing a knife for what it did to a man's insides considering the weakened condition those men were in. Isn't that so, Mr. Chandler?

CHANDLER Yes, sir.

CHIPMAN Did the men ever get anything else to eat outside of this meal?

CHANDLER A bit of meat now and then.

CHIPMAN   What sort of meat?

CHANDLER   Not very good.

CHIPMAN (*Moves to* CHANDLER)   Not very good. The prisoners had a joke about that meat, didn't they? A grim kind of a soldier joke to describe that meat from sick, dying mules and horses. They told you that the animal that meat came from— it had to be held up on its legs to be slaughtered—didn't they?

CHANDLER   Jokes of that sort—yes.

CHIPMAN   And you saw with your own eyes it was rotten, maggot-ridden meat, and that is what you meant when you said it wasn't very good, didn't you?

CHANDLER   Yes—

CHIPMAN (*Moving*)   And the conditions they were living under drove them to extreme measures in the effort to survive, isn't that so?

CHANDLER   Extreme—yes, sir.

CHIPMAN   To the point where they regarded rats as a delicacy, isn't that so?

CHANDLER   Yes, sir.

CHIPMAN   To the point that when one of them died, the others, in the desperation they had been driven to, stripped his body clean of whatever was on it in five minutes—of boots or trou-

25

sers if he had any, or bread, or greenbacks to bribe the guards —anything that might help them stay alive—isn't that correct?

CHANDLER Yes, sir.

CHIPMAN Driven in their desperation to the point of cannibalism, isn't that so?

CHANDLER Yes—

CHIPMAN You were able to establish that in your mind for a fact?

CHANDLER Yes.

CHIPMAN (*Close to the witness*) How? (*As* CHANDLER *hesitates*) As delicately as you wish, Mr. Chandler.

CHANDLER (*After a moment; with difficulty*) Well—by the condition of some bodies—very rough surgery had been performed.

CHIPMAN And so, in that place, men had been driven to the disposition of beasts—

CHANDLER Yes.

CHIPMAN (*Crosses to the map, his voice flaring*) And if I were now to sum up Andersonville as a pit—an animal pit in which men wallowed—the sick, the dying, the insane wallowing among the dead—would I exaggerate the picture of that place?

26

CHANDLER No.

CHIPMAN Concerning what you saw there . . . you submitted a report with recommendations to General Winder and your War Office, did you not?

CHANDLER I did.

CHIPMAN (*Handing over a document to* CHANDLER) This is a copy of that report?

CHANDLER (*Glancing at it and handing it back*) That is the report.

CHIPMAN Offered in evidence. (*He hands the report to* WALLACE, *who scans it and returns it to* CHIPMAN) You say in this report that Andersonville is a blot on the Confederacy. You recommend that all prisoners be transferred to other prisons without delay and that Andersonville be immediately closed down.

CHANDLER I did; yes.
        (CHIPMAN *hands the report to the* CLERK)

CLERK Exhibit one for the government.

CHIPMAN And that report was ignored, was it not? Ignored, disregarded, the condition allowed to continue—?

CHANDLER Colonel, I am not here to indict the leaders of the cause for which I fought, as plotting the murder of defenseless men.

27

CHIPMAN (*Boring in*) The report revealing how Winder and Wirz were operating that camp was ignored—

CHANDLER I have told you I could not endure Andersonville. You people act as though you were better human beings than we were!

CHIPMAN No, but our cause was. Your report was ignored?

CHANDLER Due to the crisis—the bitterness—the disorder—with General Sherman marching through Georgia burning his way—

CHIPMAN It was ignored—?

CHANDLER As your officers would have ignored it, sir, if it had been General Lee marching through Pennsylvania into New York!

WALLACE Mr. Chandler—

CHANDLER This situation is difficult for me.

WALLACE (*Stern, but not hard; he respects* CHANDLER) Nevertheless, you must answer the question. The Judge Advocate will repeat the question and you *will* answer it.

CHIPMAN Your report on Andersonville was ignored, was it not?

CHANDLER Yes, sir.

CHIPMAN Did General Winder ever express to you his disposition toward those prisoners?

28

CHANDLER   When I spoke to General Winder he had hard and bitter feelings toward them.

CHIPMAN   And how did he express those feelings?

CHANDLER   He finally said that if half of the prisoners died, there would then be twice as much room for the rest—

CHIPMAN   And the half slated for the grave were well on their way at Andersonville, weren't they? Mr. Wirz set up certain rules for that camp, rules relative to punishing prisoners attempting to escape—?

CHANDLER   Yes, sir.

CHIPMAN   His command of that camp conforming to Winder's inhuman disposition toward those men?

BAKER   I must ask the Judge Advocate what he means by that suggestive, ambiguous phrase, *conforming to.*

CHIPMAN   Withdrawn. Those rules Mr. Wirz set up at Andersonville—were they rules violating the customs of war?

CHANDLER   Well—yes.

CHIPMAN   Were they, in addition, cruel and inhuman rules?

CHANDLER   Yes.

CHIPMAN   Was Wirz the personal choice of Winder for superintendent of that camp?

CHANDLER Yes.

CHIPMAN That will be all.
 (*He crosses to his table*)

BAKER Colonel Chandler, you made a second report on Andersonville to the Confederate War Office, did you not?

CHANDLER I did, yes, sir.

BAKER That is a copy of that report?
 (*He hands the report to* SCHADE, *who shows it to* CHANDLER)

CHANDLER (*Scrutinizing it briefly and handing it back to* SCHADE)
It is.
 (SCHADE *hands it to* WALLACE, *who examines it quickly and indicates that it is acceptable*)

SCHADE Submitted for the defense—(*Handing the report to the* CLERK) Entered in evidence.

CLERK Exhibit one for the defense.

BAKER In this report—to which the Judge Advocate has failed to call attention—you recommend the dismissal of General Winder.

CHANDLER Yes.

BAKER But *not* of Captain Wirz.

CHANDLER No.

BAKER   Why not?

CHANDLER   At the time I inspected Andersonville, I saw nothing in Captain Wirz's conduct of a malignant disposition toward those men, that would have justified asking for his dismissal.

BAKER   I note in the same report that you took various prisoners aside, urging them to speak freely as to any instance of ill treatment by Captain Wirz—and they had no complaints on that score?

CHANDLER   No, sir.

BAKER   In other words, neither you nor the prisoners, who were presumably being subjected to Captain Wirz's cruel and inhuman treatment, blamed him for it, did you?

CHANDLER   No, sir.

BAKER   No more questions. Thank you, sir.

CHIPMAN   Mr. Chandler, very often, as you know, commanders are forewarned of inspection and dress up their commands in advance. Couldn't that have occurred in your case?

CHANDLER   Possibly.

CHIPMAN   And isn't it possible that the prisoners would fear the consequences of complaints against Wirz? Those men did not know you, and Wirz would still be in command after you were gone. And under those circumstances, isn't it very possible that they would not answer you truthfully?

CHANDLER   Perhaps. I did the best I could with that Andersonville situation—

CHIPMAN (*Inwardly raging; silent for a moment*)   Did Wirz do the best he could? (*Rises and crosses to the witness*) In spite of Winder's orders, couldn't he have chosen to . . . (*Frustrated*) . . . there are ways!

BAKER   Ways of doing what? Evading the orders of his superior? What is the Judge Advocate suggesting?

CHIPMAN (*Crosses to his table, sits*)   Withdrawn. That will be all, thank you, Mr. Chandler.

WALLACE   If there are no other questions the witness may step down. The Court thanks the witness.
   (CHANDLER *goes.* CHIPMAN's *tone is becoming more peremptory*)

CHIPMAN   We call Dr. John C. Bates to the stand.

LIEUTENANT   Dr. John C. Bates.
   (BATES *comes in and is sworn. He is a type of country doctor; an honest man with small vanities*)

CHIPMAN   Dr. Bates, were you in the service of the Confederate Army during the year 1864?

BATES   Yes, sir.

CHIPMAN   Were you at any time inside the Andersonville stockade?

BATES   Yes, sir. For about eight months during '64.

CHIPMAN   In what capacity were you there?

BATES   As a medical officer—assigned to the camp by the Surgeon General. I can't say I asked for it.

CHIPMAN   I suppose not. Describe your activity there as a physician.

BATES   Writing prescriptions for drugs that were not available, amputations of limbs due to gangrene—quite a lot of that—and certifying the dead in my section each morning—quite a lot of that too.

CHIPMAN   Did you in the course of your stay there make any estimate of the rate of death at that place?

BATES   I did; yes, sir. I had always kept a ledger book covering the ailments and treatment of my patients in civil life—farmers—their families—their horses too. And I decided to keep some sort of a record in that camp . . . because I was deeply shocked by that place when I came there.

CHIPMAN   Please tell the Court what your estimate of the death rate was.

BATES   In the spring months it averaged fifty, sixty, seventy men a day . . . in spells of extreme heat during the summer reaching a hundred men a day. More in May than in April, more in June than in May, and in July, August, September, three thousand men a month were dying.

CHIPMAN   What were the principal causes for that high rate of death?

BATES   The lack of sanitary facilities—the lack of exercise—the anemia of the men from lack of food rendering them subject to fatal illness from the slightest abrasion or infection—the lack of medical supplies.

CHIPMAN   And, Dr. Bates, in your professional opinion, how many of the thousands who died there would have lived if conditions had at least been sanitary?

BATES   I would estimate—seventy-five to eighty per cent.

CHIPMAN   Ten to eleven thousand of those fourteen thousand men—

BATES   Yes, sir.

CHIPMAN   Can you think of sanitary measures which, if taken at Andersonville, would have saved lives—?

BATES   A number; yes.

CHIPMAN   Were such measures suggested to Wirz?

BATES   Yes, sir. By myself—perhaps others.

CHIPMAN   And what did he say?

BATES   He said I was a doctor and didn't understand his difficulties running a huge camp like that. He was downright incoherent—damned me for a Yankee sympathizer—and cursed me out in English, German and some other foreign dialect—

WIRZ   French. That was French, Dr. Bates—

BATES   French, eh?

WALLACE   (*Brings down the gavel*)   For your own good, Mr. Wirz, keep in mind that your situation here is not amusing.

WIRZ   No, sir—and I can't explain it to myself or to the Court, why I have this feeling to laugh, hearing how I killed all those men. Perhaps the Court can explain it.

WALLACE   Do not play the clown here . . . Continue, Colonel.

CHIPMAN   Only one more question—on that not so humorous occasion when you spoke to Wirz and he complained to you that his job was difficult . . . did you understand him to mean his job was difficult administratively or difficult— (*Searching for his thought*)—humanly?

BATES   Mr. Wirz dwelt on *his* difficulties—not the men's.

CHIPMAN   That will be all, Doctor. Thank you.
   (*He sits*)

BAKER   Dr. Bates, you regard yourself as a fair-minded man, don't you?

BATES   I do.

BAKER   The fact that you dislike Captain Wirz has not influenced your testimony here in any way, has it?

BATES   No, it has not—

BAKER   But you *did* dislike him, didn't you?

BATES   Not so as to influence my professional objective judgment—

BAKER   I now address myself to that professional *objective* judgment, Doctor—strictly to that. So far as you know, by whose authority was the amount of food per prisoner decided on?

BATES   By the Commissary General at Richmond, I believe.

BAKER   And not by Captain Wirz. And by whose authority was the amount and type of medical supply to the camp decided on?

BATES   The Surgeon General.

BAKER   And not by Captain Wirz. He was responsible neither for the lack of food nor the inadequate medical supplies.

BATES   I would have to agree.

BAKER   You would have to agree. You don't want to agree but you would have to agree, is that what you mean, Dr. Bates? You seem to have found Captain Wirz rather calloused toward the condition of the prisoners.

BATES   That was my honest impression.

BAKER Well, we are all entitled to our honest impressions. I recall you saying a few minutes ago that you were shocked at the high rate of death in the Andersonville prison when you came there.

BATES Deeply shocked.

BAKER (*With a show of sympathy*) One can understand how unnerving it must have been. That was in what month by the way?

BATES In February.

BAKER And you had to face that unnerving scene day after day and month after month—it's difficult to understand how you could do that.

BATES Well, sir, I had to steel myself and gradually the shock of it became endurable.

BAKER I'm curious, Doctor—how gradually did your feeling of shock lessen? For example, how did you react to the dying— by June, let us say?

BATES Not as much.

BAKER And by September?

BATES Far less—

BAKER So that by September, when, as you said, three thousand men a month were dying, you hardly reacted at all—?

BATES I meant—I had grown accustomed—

BAKER (*Gesturing in the direction of* WIRZ) Of course you had. Any human being to save his sanity would have had to do that. So Captain Wirz's "callousness" in that place wasn't so strange after all, was it?

BATES (*Rattled*) Well—my impression of Mr. Wirz remains the same, despite that.

BAKER Thank you, that will be all.
  (BAKER *returns to the defense table;* CHIPMAN *comes forward*)

CHIPMAN (*Sharp*) Dr. Bates, do you remember one single instance, in conversing with Wirz, when he expressed any criticism of the orders or disposition of his superior?

BAKER Objection. I find that a strange question to be asked by a counsel for the War Department, himself a soldier. Is it being held against Captain Wirz that he did not make a public judgment of the motives of his military superior?

WALLACE (*Considering. The question has implications and there is a noticeable stir among the* JUDGES. *They confer briefly*) The Court must agree Wirz was not bound to comment on the order of his military superior.

CHIPMAN (*Facing* JUDGES, *driving*) If the Court please, we are concerned here with the frame of mind of a man carrying out his superior's inhuman design. We are bound to explore his thinking when he obeyed those orders—

BAKER (*Rising*) His thinking when he obeyed those orders? And if he did not like those orders what was he supposed to do? Disobey them? If conscience is the measure by which soldiers obey or disobey orders, one can hardly condemn the Army officers who went over to the Confederacy, since they did so on the ground of conscience—(*The gavel comes down*) And on that ground Robert E. Lee deserves a monument—

WALLACE (*Obviously perturbed*) That will be all, Mr. Baker ... (*To* CHIPMAN) I am certain it was not in the mind of the Judge Advocate to raise the issue of disobedience to a superior officer—

CHIPMAN (*Crosses slowly to table, sits, inwardly resisting the Court*) Under certain circumstances that issue may require consideration—

WALLACE (*With great deliberation—cueing, ordering and warning* CHIPMAN *at the same time*) The Court is not, of course, suggesting the line of inquiry the Judge Advocate is to take here. But the Court will say that it is disposed to draw its own inference as to a criminal design from evidence of the defendant's words and acts—and not from an examination of moral factors which can drop us into a bottomless pool of philosophic debate ... I am certain the Judge Advocate will agree and that he will withdraw that question as to whether or not Wirz criticized his superior officer.

CHIPMAN (*His glance travels slowly and sullenly down the line of* JUDGES, *fighting them, and then*—) The question is withdrawn. (*Moves to the witness; in a temper*) Dr. Bates, you never grew so accustomed to that place as to forget your human obligation to those men, did you? You made it your daily business to bring in food from the outside for those starving men, didn't you?

BATES   Of course.

CHIPMAN   And there was plenty of food in the region of Andersonville to draw from, if Wirz had wished to bring it in—the yield of grain and vegetables in the region was considerable, wasn't it?

BAKER   Is Dr. Bates put forward as qualified to testify on the agricultural situation?

CHIPMAN   Withdrawn! If the Court please, we wish to change the order of appearance of witnesses. We would like at this time to call a witness qualified to speak with accuracy on the available food supply in the vicinity of Andersonville.

WALLACE   Does defense counsel offer objection to a change in the order of the government witnesses?

BAKER   Not at all.

CHIPMAN   Ambrose Spencer to the stand!

WALLACE   The Court thanks you, Dr. Bates. You may step down.

LIEUTENANT   Ambrose Spencer!

BAKER   (*Cool and amused; pointing up* CHIPMAN's *failure to thank the witness*)   *We* thank the witness.

CHIPMAN   Thank you, Dr. Bates! (BATES *exits.* SPENCER *enters, is sworn in and takes the stand. A somewhat glib, unctuous, coarse country squire type.* CHIPMAN'S *questioning is now more impatient; he treads on the tail of* SPENCER'S *answers*) Mr. Spencer, tell us where you reside.

SPENCER   I reside in the town of Americus, in Sumter County, Georgia—

CHIPMAN   Your occupation?

SPENCER   I operate a plantation in that county—corn, cotton, tobacco and—

CHIPMAN   Is that plantation in proximity to the site of Andersonville?

SPENCER   Practically bordering it.

CHIPMAN (*Pacing*)   You are therefore in a position to know as well as any man the yield of grain and vegetables in the region of Andersonville.

SPENCER   I would say so.

CHIPMAN   How would you estimate yields for the years 1863 and 1864?

SPENCER (*With obvious satisfaction*)   Both good years. Sumter and the adjoining county, Macon, I may point out, are part of a very productive area—sometimes termed the garden of the Confederacy, and—

CHIPMAN   Yes, yes. We will have some details as to the yield.

SPENCER   Corn averaged about eight bushels to the acre, wheat six. That is the general average but we have land in Sumter County producing thirty-five—

CHIPMAN   And as to vegetables?

SPENCER   We had an uncommon amount during the war since there was so little cotton planted and all the ground was pretty well planted in provisions.

CHIPMAN   And, if Mr. Wirz had solicited food for the prisoners from the farms and plantations in the area—what in your judgment would have happened?

SPENCER   He would have gotten it.
          (*As* SPENCER *goes on,* WIRZ *sits up.* BAKER *restrains him*)

CHIPMAN   What makes you so certain of that?

SPENCER   The proof, sir, is that without it being solicited, there were people in the vicinity who came forward and made an effort to get food into that camp. In one case a group of women in Americus, including my wife, made that attempt.

CHIPMAN   Tell the Court what happened on that occasion.

SPENCER   Well, sir, the ladies thought it would be the Christian thing to do, having heard that the prisoners were doing so poorly. They obtained enough food through contributions to fill four wagons and had them driven—

CHIPMAN   How large were those wagons?

SPENCER   The largest farm wagons they could find—each requiring four to six horses to pull it.

CHIPMAN   Making a load of how much food for those men?

SPENCER   Oh, maybe twenty tons.

CHIPMAN   Continue, sir.

SPENCER   They had those wagons driven up to the gate of the stockade. Mr. Wirz was at the gate when those ladies arrived. He would not permit the food to be brought in— He cursed those women. He told them they were giving aid and comfort to the enemy—that Yankee soldiers were unlawfully invading—looting the South—that those women were traitors—and worse. He used the violentest and profanest language I have ever heard in a man's mouth. He said if he had his way he would have a certain kind of a house built for those women and he would put them all in there where the Confederate soldiers would teach them loyalty in a hurry and teach it to them in a way they wouldn't forget—

CHIPMAN   We understand the remark, sir. And those ladies were turned away by Mr. Wirz from giving food to those starving men—

SPENCER   They were turned away and they wept.

CHIPMAN   And if Mr. Wirz had solicited food—on Christian grounds and on behalf of the good name of the Confederacy —you think that would have brought in large amounts of food—?

43

SPENCER   I am certain the people of Georgia would have re-
sponded—

CHIPMAN   You were acquainted with the defendant, were you
not?

SPENCER   Knew him quite well.

CHIPMAN   And you knew General Winder—

SPENCER   Knew him too.

CHIPMAN   And from your knowledge, what can you tell us
about the disposition of General Winder toward those prisoners?

SPENCER   When he came there once, Winder said that the
Yankees had come South to take possession of the land and
that he was endeavoring to satisfy them by giving them each
a small plot—pointing to the grave site.

CHIPMAN   And did you ever hear Wirz speak along the same
lines?

SPENCER   I can tell you that he stated that he wished all those
men in hell—that he boasted he was killing more Yankees at
Andersonville than Lee was at Richmond—

CHIPMAN   You heard those remarks—?

SPENCER   Yes—to wipe out those men. That was the scheme.

44

CHIPMAN Thank you.
    (*He goes to his table*)

WIRZ (*As* CHIPMAN *finishes*) That was my scheme, you say?
To wipe out those men? On my head all those men?
    (*He rises,* BAKER *and* SCHADE *come to him*)

WALLACE (*Overlapping*) Mr. Wirz . . . !

WIRZ I was a man like other men—

WALLACE (*Overlapping*) Counsel, you will restrain—

WIRZ (*Breaking away from* BAKER *and* SCHADE *and crossing to*
JUDGES' *table*) Who will understand? An ordinary man like
me—assigned—!

WALLACE (*Overlapping*) Guards!
    (*The two* GUARDS, *the* LIEUTENANT, CAPTAIN WILLIAMS *and*
    DR. FORD *move in on* WIRZ)

WIRZ The drummer boys I saved—and now—(*In a drawn-out
cry*)—I am surrounded!
    (*As the* GUARDS *reach for him, he slumps down in a faint.
    He is carried to the sofa*)

FORD (*To* SCHADE) A bottle of brandy, in the bag.

BAKER I ask for a postponement.

WALLACE Dr. Ford?

45

FORD A fainting spell from which he recovers. He lacks strength and suffers from strain but should be well enough to continue —I suppose.

(WIRZ *comes to consciousness, raising himself to lean on an elbow, watching*)

WALLACE This trial must go on—

BAKER If the Court please—

WALLACE It is no use, Mr. Baker—

BAKER The open bias of the witness is a case in point. I need not remind the Court of the bitterness in our time—

WALLACE It is no use, Mr. Baker—

BAKER Even the sight of a tattered Confederate blouse is a cause for riot in the streets. The very air is charged.

WALLACE (*The case is beginning to coil about him*) We are not empowered to move this trial into the next century— This trial will continue. You will make clear to the defendant that should there be another demonstration here he will be tried *in absentia*—

WIRZ *In absentia*. Latin for absence. I understand all languages but the language of this trial—

BAKER The Court has suffered sufficient provocation to send Captain Wirz from this courtroom but I suggest it does not—

WALLACE (*In a cold, deadly tone*) You suggest we do not—

46

Foreground: Herbert Berghof and Albert Dekker, as WIRZ and BAKER

BAKER Since it is not he alone in this room who is stripped down to naked hatred and anger—

WALLACE Counsel will cross-examine or stand down.

BAKER Counsel will cross-examine! Mr. Spencer, you don't regard yourself as prejudiced against Captain Wirz, do you?

SPENCER I don't.

BAKER Then why have you chosen to leave out of that touching tale about those women bringing food to that camp the fact that General Winder was there at the time and that it was he who ordered that food kept out?

SPENCER Why?

BAKER Yes, why. You were at the main gate of the camp together with other civilians and you heard General Winder say loudly and emphatically that that food was not to be brought in—

SPENCER Wirz wouldn't have tried in any case. I know that man.

BAKER Answer the question— Why didn't you say so?

SPENCER I wasn't asked.

BAKER You weren't asked. Motion to dismiss Mr. Spencer's testimony as irrelevant in that it offers nothing other than that Captain Wirz was carrying out a direct order.

47

CHIPMAN   Move to deny.

BAKER   Will the Judge Advocate offer a ground for denial? Is he saying that Captain Wirz should have defied that direct order of General Winder's?

CHIPMAN   Will you deny that was an inhuman order?

BAKER   Which he should have disobeyed?

WALLACE   Defense motion is denied.

BAKER   (*With restrained, deliberate fury*)   Of course denied. It is now plain enough why the government has chosen to try Captain Wirz on a conspiracy charge. On that charge the accused may be convicted without any direct evidence against him—

WALLACE (*Rising*)   Mr. Baker!
   (WALLACE, *half-risen, remains in that position as* BAKER *continues, his eyes fixed on* BAKER, *head cocked as if to make sure he will not miss one word*)

BAKER (*Going on*)   —and if there is a conspiracy, it is one directed against Captain Wirz. I say now that the motives which bring Wirz to trial here dishonor the government of the United States; and that contradicting its own military code— the Army will have this man though he was only doing his proper duty.

WALLACE   Are you through, Mr. Baker?

BAKER   I am through, sir.

48

WALLACE You have been in contempt since the beginning of that outburst. The Court will consider a formal charge against you. You are dismissed from this proceeding forthwith, and will immediately leave this room.

BAKER Let Captain Wirz be without counsel—so this trial may be judged for what it is—

WALLACE (*Not waiting for* BAKER *to finish*) Guards—escort Mr. Baker from the room.
    (BAKER *starts for the door. His manner is cool. The* JUDGES *look at one another and then toward* CHIPMAN. *The dilemma is theirs*)

WIRZ (*Crying out*) I appeal to the Court! I will have no counsel—(*And then, almost with satisfaction*) No counsel then. It makes no difference.

CHIPMAN (*Swiftly*) I respectfully request the Court . . . (BAKER *halts on hearing* CHIPMAN *begin to speak*) The Court has borne the provocative behavior of defense counsel with the utmost patience—I request that Mr. Baker be allowed to purge himself of contempt if he so wishes. (*Making his meaning clear despite the elaborate phrasing*) I pray that the magnanimity of the Court extend itself so that not even in the wildest misrepresentation of this trial may it be said this defendant was denied counsel of his choice.

WALLACE (*After a pause*) Mr. Baker. For the single reason that Mr. Wirz may have counsel of his choice, you may now purge yourself of contempt if you so wish. You may do so by recanting those remarks impugning the integrity of the gov-

49

ernment and Army of the United States, by apologizing to the Court and by giving us your oath such outbursts will not occur again.

BAKER (*With great deliberateness, aware of the face-saving involved*)   I do so recant and apologize and give my oath that I will not hereafter impugn the fairness of the Court or the motives of the government and Army of the United States. (*He crosses to the table and sits*)

WALLACE The Judge Advocate will—(*Notices the witness*) Are we through with this witness? (*Both lawyers indicate that they are*) The Court thanks the witness and he may step down. (SPENCER *exits*) Call your next witness, Colonel. (*During the following speech, as the lights begin to dim out,* CHIPMAN's *voice is heard, dying away*)

CHIPMAN On the specification that the defendant did keep in barbarously close confinement soldiers numbering at times forty thousand men without adequate shelter from the rain and heat of summer and the cold of winter, we call . . .

The Lights Fade Out

Scene Two

A week later. The weather continues hot.

As the lights come up to full, the witness, JAMES DAVIDSON, *is in the chair, and we hear* CHIPMAN'S *voice coming back as he examines* DAVIDSON. CHIPMAN *is examining him, with a driving, desperate quality, his tunic unbuttoned, collar open.*

DAVIDSON *is young. War and prison experience haunt his face. He is feeble and ill at ease and his postwar motley costume of Army tunic and civilian trousers hangs loosely on his gaunt frame. One may imagine how deeply he longs for a quiet, rest-ful place.*

CHIPMAN (*Close to the witness; his voice rasping*) Now, Mr. Davidson, Captain Wirz *knew* the dogs tore and killed prisoners of war?

DAVIDSON It was commonly known, yes, sir.

CHIPMAN Knew it, and permitted it, and as far as you know, never took steps to put an end to that practice—(BAKER *starts to object*) Withdrawn! Mr. Davidson, during the time you were a prisoner at Andersonville, did you ever see a man torn by dogs—I mean on an occasion when Wirz was present?

DAVIDSON Yes, sir.

CHIPMAN Tell us about it.

51

DAVIDSON (*Slowly; too slowly for* CHIPMAN) Saw that after tunneling out of the stockade with another prisoner. We got maybe fifteen miles from the camp when the dogs treed us. The guards ordered us down. And I saw those dogs tear my companion.

CHIPMAN And Captain Wirz was there, wasn't he?

DAVIDSON Captain Wirz rode up a minute after that pack of dogs had treed us, yelling, "Get those Yankee bastards"—beggin' your pardon.

CHIPMAN And he was present while those dogs were tearing your companion?

DAVIDSON While they were tearing him, yes, sir.

CHIPMAN And what was Wirz doing while they tore him—?

DAVIDSON Damning that man to hell—beg—his eyes starting out of his head—like a fit was on him.

CHIPMAN Can you recall another instance—an instance where—

WALLACE (*His irritation is obvious*) Before we hear the answer we will ask the Judge Advocate if he expects, as he stated yesterday, to conclude his case today—

CHIPMAN We shall make every effort to conclude—
    (*They are fighting now*)

WALLACE The Court does not wish to exclude pertinent testimony but we have heard a great number of the former Andersonville prisoners testify—

CHIPMAN I am now trying to establish Mr. Wirz's attitude when he was present on occasions where extreme cruelty was practiced— The Court will understand that we call only those witnesses we think necessary . . .

WALLACE Of course—

CHIPMAN —and we cannot altogether control the time required for thorough examination of witnesses—

WALLACE Naturally. However, the Court does not consider it necessary to hear further evidence corroborating facts alleged many times over. Will the government conclude this afternoon?

CHIPMAN We will conclude this afternoon, sir.

WALLACE Continue, Colonel.

CHIPMAN Mr. Davidson, the question is, did you know of any instance where an escaped prisoner was tracked down and actually *killed* by dogs? And again, I am referring to an instance when Wirz was present. (DAVIDSON *does not answer*) Did you hear my question, Mr. Davidson?

DAVIDSON Yes, sir.

CHIPMAN Well?

DAVIDSON   I—want to forget about that place, Colonel.

CHIPMAN (*Curtly*)   State the circumstances.

DAVIDSON   Was this time a man from my prison squad escaped. Tunneling through to the outside one night. But then we heard the rumor he'd been captured by the dogs.

CHIPMAN   You actually saw that man being brought back to the stockade—

DAVIDSON   Yes, sir. First through the gate is Captain Wirz on that big gray he rode and then come two guards and this man between them . . . And they was holding him . . . and letting him go once he was inside that gate . . . He fell down . . . his legs was torn and his throat laid open. His flesh torn about the legs and his neck bloody.

CHIPMAN   And did he get up or did he lie there?

DAVIDSON   Made as if to get up and then lay back. Didn't move after that.

CHIPMAN   And where was Wirz during all this time?

DAVIDSON   Right there.

CHIPMAN   Right *where?*

DAVIDSON   Like I said, sir—

CHIPMAN   We will hear it again, *please,* Mr. Davidson.

54

DAVIDSON Like I said, he rode in as this man fell down. Captain Wirz rode around him looking down at him, reining in his horse which was skittering and rearing—that was a horse with a temper—then rode back through the gate.

CHIPMAN That will be all. Thank you.

BAKER (*His manner is gentle, in conscious contrast to* CHIPMAN's) Mr. Davidson, we will not detain you long, sir. In that first instance you have described—when you made your escape attempt—you say Captain Wirz cursed, urging on those dogs, that were tearing your companion?

DAVIDSON Yes, sir.

BAKER Tell me, Mr. Davidson, at any time in your career as a soldier—did you ever yell—"Get those Rebel bastards"?

DAVIDSON I guess so.

BAKER And what was it that Captain Wirz yelled—?

DAVIDSON "Get—those—Yankee—" But that was different.

BAKER How different?

DAVIDSON He meant for those dogs to tear that man, and I saw them do that.

BAKER You were close enough to see that—

DAVIDSON Yes—

55

BAKER   Well—*how* close, would you say?

DAVIDSON   Ten, fifteen feet away maybe. No more 'n from here to there.

BAKER   And how was it, Mr. Davidson, those dogs did not tear you? (DAVIDSON *stares at* BAKER *in shocked, puzzled silence*) How do you account for that? (DAVIDSON *shakes his head inarticulately*) Can you think of any reason, Mr. Davidson?
     (*After a pause*)

DAVIDSON   I wouldn't know why, sir.

BAKER   Now, since you admit those ferocious dogs didn't attack *you,* shall I understand you were completely unhurt when you were brought back to the camp?

DAVIDSON (*Slowly*)   No, sir.

BAKER   You were bruised some, as a result of rushing pell-mell through the swamps, weren't you?

DAVIDSON   Yes.

BAKER   Bloodied a bit, too?

DAVIDSON   Some. From all that running and stumbling against rocks—

56

BAKER Yes. And from bramble bushes and whipping branches and dead cypress limbs, some of them as pointed as knives?

DAVIDSON Yes, sir.

BAKER It would bruise and bloody any man, trying to beat a pursuit through a Georgia swamp, wouldn't it?

DAVIDSON I guess so.

BAKER So in that second instance you spoke of, when you saw a man brought back to the stockade—couldn't those marks on him that you say were caused by the dogs—couldn't they have been caused by his rushing headlong through the swamps, as yours were?

DAVIDSON That man was torn by dogs—

BAKER Well, now you didn't *see* him being torn by dogs, did you, Mr. Davidson?

DAVIDSON It was commonly known that the dogs—

BAKER Many things are commonly known, sir. Could you identify the bruises on this man as being indisputably caused by dogs?

DAVIDSON (*Feebly stubborn*) He was bit by the dogs and he died—

BAKER (*Shrugging*) Possibly. How long did you remain at that spot after this man—you don't happen to know his name, do you?

DAVIDSON   No, sir.

BAKER   How long did you remain there after that man fell down?

DAVIDSON   Three—five minutes.

BAKER   And did you have occasion to look that way later?

DAVIDSON   Some time later—yes.

BAKER   And was he still lying there?

DAVIDSON   No, sir—taken off to the dead house—

BAKER   Or to the sick ward? (*Waiting*) Mr. Davidson, you can't say this man died as a result of being mutilated by dogs and you can't identify this man, is that correct?

DAVIDSON   (*To* WALLACE)   Sir, please. I got to go back home.

BAKER   And Captain Wirz riding around that man . . . without a word—that sounds mighty unfeeling. You wouldn't know whether he notified the guard at the gate to have that man moved, would you?

DAVIDSON   I got to go home.

BAKER   Thank you, Mr. Davidson. That will be all.

CHIPMAN   (*Crosses to the witness; his temper is barely under control*)   Mr. Davidson, didn't Wirz openly show his contempt and hatred for those men torn and killed by dogs?
        (DAVIDSON *glances toward* WIRZ)

58

DAVIDSON (*Wretchedly*) I don't know.

CHIPMAN You don't know? With Wirz coldly sitting his horse—indifferent to that man brought back to die—

DAVIDSON I can't say for sure now how he felt—

CHIPMAN (*Hardly waiting for the answer; starting to lose control*) But those were the marks of teeth and claws that you identified on that man, weren't they?

DAVIDSON I guess so—

CHIPMAN (*Shouting*) You were quite sure of all that at one time. You also said that he died—that the flies set on his face and he didn't move to brush them off—

DAVIDSON I don't remember—

CHIPMAN And Captain Wirz looking on—looking on—that dying man.

DAVIDSON I—I—

CHIPMAN All I am asking you to repeat is what you already have sworn to under oath—that his attitude was monstrously cold and indifferent to those dying men!

DAVIDSON (*High*) Let me be, Colonel!

CHIPMAN Mr. Davidson, I must warn you—!

DAVIDSON (*At absolute pitch*) I got to forget that place—!

59

CHIPMAN (*Shouting*) Or has it been suggested to you that you forget that place—!

WALLACE Colonel Chipman! (CHIPMAN *turns away, crosses to the table and sits, fighting for control*) I think the witness is through. (*Gently—pointedly looking at* CHIPMAN) Are you now ill, Mr. Davidson?

DAVIDSON (*Steps off the podium*) Yes, sir. I got pains—

WALLACE You have told us about that incident as well as you can now recall it, is that correct?

DAVIDSON Yes, sir.

WALLACE How old are you, Mr. Davidson?

DAVIDSON Nineteen, sir.

WALLACE I believe you said you fought with the Second Vermont Cavalry.

DAVIDSON (*He straightens*) The Second Vermont Cavalry, sir. We turned their flank many times.

WALLACE You may now go home and the Court wishes you Godspeed in recovering good health and in forgetting what you have endured in war and in prison.

DAVIDSON Yes, sir. Thank you sir. (*Starts out and stops; looking uncertainly from* CHIPMAN *to* BAKER, *searching himself*) Could be those dogs didn't tear me for the same reason Daniel was not tore in the lion's den. There was many died in that place. Many died. I hear those dogs baying at night. I hear voices cry out "Help, help" and no one to help. Many died. Many, many died.

CHIPMAN (*After a silence; terribly strained*)   I apologize to the witness.

DAVIDSON   Yes, sir.
     (*He exits*)

WALLACE (*With deliberateness*)   The weather continues hot and we have been at this trial longer than anticipated. I will ascribe tempers to the heat. Call your next witness, Colonel.

CHIPMAN   Joseph Achuff to the stand—

WALLACE   Is Mr. Achuff called to testify on the specification that dogs attacked escaping prisoners?

CHIPMAN   Yes, sir.

WALLACE   The Court considers it unnecessary to hear further testimony on that specification; it has been amply testified to by previous witnesses.

CHIPMAN   If the Court please—

WALLACE   That is the judgment of the Court. Call your next witness, Colonel.
     (CHIPMAN *strides to the prosecution table*)

CHIPMAN (*To* HOSMER)   Who next?

HOSMER   Hardy.

CHIPMAN   Baker will roast him and toss him back to me well done.

HOSMER (*With meaning; they have talked of this before*)   He won't roast Gray—

CHIPMAN   So Gray is here . . . I won't put him on—(*To the Court*) As our final witness on the specification that the defendant caused the death of prisoners by direct order, we call Jasper Culver to the stand.
 (WIRZ *reacts*)

LIEUTENANT   Jasper Culver!
 (CULVER *enters. There is a punch-drunk suggestion in his walk. He smiles uncertainly. He is sworn in. As* CULVER *gets into his story, he will begin to act it out*)

CHIPMAN   Mr. Culver, what was your regiment and when were you captured and brought to Andersonville?

CULVER   I was connected with the Sixty-seventh New York Infantry—and was captured and brought to Andersonville in March, 1864.

CHIPMAN   Did you ever see a prisoner of war killed? Inside the stockade?

CULVER   I did.

CHIPMAN   Who killed him?

CULVER   The guard.

CHIPMAN   And did that guard do so on his own or because of a direct order?

62

CULVER   He was given a direct order to kill him.

CHIPMAN   By whom?

CULVER   By Captain Wirz.

CHIPMAN   And where did that killing take place?

CULVER   At the deadline.

CHIPMAN   Who was the man you saw killed?

CULVER   We called him Chickamauga. Because he had lost a leg
in that battle and because he had lost his memory there. So we
called him by that name—Chickamauga.

CHIPMAN   And why did Chickamauga want to cross that line?

CULVER   He wished to lie down under a pine tree, he said, because a long time ago—but not that he could remember where
—he had laid down under a pine tree. "I can't remember
nothing before Chickamauga" is what he said to the guard . . .

CHIPMAN   State the circumstances—when did this occur?

CULVER   It was in the early fall, I believe . . . I remember the
smell of burning leaves.

CHIPMAN   Continue, sir.

CULVER   I watched Chickamauga go toward the deadline and
called to him to stop, but he went on as if not hearing. At the
line he shouted to the sentry to let him cross, but the sentry

waved him back. Chickamauga then began to move up and down the line, hopping back and forth on his one leg, begging to be let out of the stockade for ten minutes. The guard let him stay on the line but he was nervous and telling Chickamauga to get—(*He laughs*)—back and Chickamauga laughed. And then Chickamauga, he said for the guard to tell Captain Wirz that he knew of a plot whereby all the men would escape and he would tell Captain Wirz about that plot in exchange for being let out a few minutes, and with that the guard called for the Captain to come. And Wirz came. And when Chickamauga saw Wirz he made the Captain promise to let him rest a few minutes under that pine tree if he tells him that plot and the Captain says he will do that, and then Chickamauga he says to the Captain, "I will tell you that plot to escape. Here it is in a nutshell. Why, you know Uncle Billy Sherman in his white socks is marching through Georgia and what he is going to do is blast Andersonville open from the outside and that is how the men will get free." And Wirz began to rave and he said to Chickamauga, "I am going to give you a pass to hell," and Chickamauga said, "You can't give me no pass to hell on account I'm in hell now." And Captain Wirz turned to the guard and said, "Get that man back across the line or shoot him." The guard said, "I can't shoot no cripple." And Captain Wirz said, "If you don't obey I will have you court-martialed." And the next thing the guard shot Chickamauga and he fell over the deadline. Done for.

CHIPMAN   That will be all.

BAKER   Mr. Culver, I am thinking of how accurately you told that story. You remember the details down to the exact words said back and forth. That sense of detail makes you a most excellent witness.

CULVER   Thank you, sir.

BAKER   And one might add—it is also the characteristic of a good soldier—which I am sure you were before Andersonville—

CULVER   (*Echoing in mingled emotions of pain and pride*)   Before Andersonville!

BAKER   When you were in the line.

CULVER   (*Beginning to chant*)   In the line! Antietam Bridge, Chancellorsville and Stafford Court House—

BAKER   And you must remember the nighttime bivouacs, around the fires, listening to the sentries—

CULVER   Around the fires! Hearing them calling through the dark, "All is well"—post one to post two, "All is well"—

BAKER   And that outpost line—that of course was a line which a man dare not cross on pain of being shot by the sentries—

CULVER   On pain of being shot by the sentries!— And "Who goes there?" is the cry, "Who goes there?" "Who goes—"

BAKER   And of course you can tell us why such lines are set up by commanding officers, Mr. Culver. As you remember it, sir, by the book.

CULVER   (*Very correct; sounding out*)   By the book, sir— And that is for the order and safety of the camp.

BAKER   And inside the stockade at Andersonville—were there signs posted warning men not to cross the line?

CULVER   (*With an air of modesty*)   I recall some—yes, Counsel, there were.

BAKER   That story you told about Chickamauga. With the great interest people have in anecdotes about the war, you have undoubtedly had occasion to tell it a number of times already, Mr. Culver, haven't you?

CULVER   I have been requested to tell it a number of times.

BAKER   I'll wager you could tell it a hundred times and it would come out exactly as you told it today—

CULVER   A thousand times, Counsel, and it would come out the same way.

BAKER   And always told with great effect, I imagine.

CULVER   With great effect, yes, sir.

BAKER   It would hardly be as effective if Captain Wirz did not come out the villain of the piece, would it?

CULVER   Hardly—(*Starting; staring at* BAKER. *A grim, sober expression coming into his face*) You wish to make a fool of me, Counsel. I'm not lying—

BAKER   (*In a sad anger*)   No, Mr. Culver, you are not. A man can't help it if fables grow in his head, can he?

CULVER   No, he—*fables?*— I don't know what you're talking about—!

66

BAKER (*Moving to address the Court*) I'm looking for facts and I'm hunting for them through fairy tales of good and evil— Mr. Culver, you say you heard Captain Wirz say, "Get that man back across the line or shoot him." Didn't Wirz actually say, "*For God's sakes,* get that man back across the line or you will have to shoot him"?

CULVER It is frozen into my memory as I have said it—

BAKER And when Chickamauga said, "I am in hell now," didn't Wirz say, "You and I both"—"You and I both are in hell"—as indeed they both were?

CULVER I have said it as I remember it—!

BAKER As you need to remember it. That will be all, Mr. Culver, thank you. Move to dismiss all counts under this specification since the deadline was a proper military line required for the order and safety of that camp.

CHIPMAN (*Moving to the map*) It was not a purely military line! Mr. Culver, look at the map. Where the stream entered the camp under the west wall. There! What was that water like?

CULVER (*Dazed*) Somewhat fast-flowing, yes, sir.

CHIPMAN Was it drinkable?

CULVER Somewhat drinkable, yes, sir. (*Pointing to* BAKER) That man there!—

CHIPMAN And inside the deadline, what was the water like there?

67

CULVER Not fittin' to drink, no, sir.

CHIPMAN It was by that time filthy and clogged with waste matter—driving the men to do *what*—?

CULVER To try for a drink near the west wall.

CHIPMAN (*Circling the witness*) And they had to wade waist-deep through that swamp to get that drink of water, didn't they?

CHIPMAN Waist-deep and further—

CHIPMAN And when they succeeded in getting to that water, what did the guards do?

CULVER Opened fire on us—yes—

CHIPMAN Killing men?

CULVER Killing and wounding—yes, yes!

CHIPMAN Killing and wounding for a drink of water! And Wirz knew that and he let those men get shot down, didn't he?— And Counsel calls that a purely military line! Move to deny defense motion as to that deadline in that it was clearly part of the cold, inhuman design of that camp.

BAKER Inhuman?

CHIPMAN Yes.

BAKER Immoral?

CHIPMAN Yes.

WIRZ   I can explain—

BAKER   (*Gesturing to quiet* WIRZ)   Will the Judge Advocate openly and finally admit his belief that Captain Wirz's duty was to make a moral, not a military choice?

CHIPMAN   The *human* choice.

WALLACE   This arguing over an irrelevant issue becomes intolerable—parties are warned. Defense motion denied. (BAKER *sits down;* WALLACE's *tone is deadly*)   The Judge Advocate will now state the connection between the moral issue and the charge of conspiracy.

CHIPMAN   (*After a pause; tired*)   The Judge Advocate will not attempt to make that connection.

WALLACE   Thank you, Mr. Culver, you may stand down. (CULVER *exits*)   If you have concluded your case, Colonel, we will now adjourn until tomorrow morning, at which time the defense will be ready—

CHIPMAN   We may wish to call further witnesses—

WALLACE   If so they will be witnesses bringing in new criminal evidence. I say *new* criminal evidence in the precise legal meaning of the term, bearing *directly* on the charge of conspiracy. I hope that is understood.

CHIPMAN   Yes, sir.

WALLACE   The Court stands adjourned.
     (*General   exit.   Opposing   counsel   remain   in   the*

room. BAKER *takes his and* SCHADE'S *hats from the rack and gathers up his papers)*

BAKER   The choices in this world are bitter, Colonel, aren't they? On the one hand to follow your decent instincts and on the other— Tell me, if you can, Colonel, how does your role in this room differ from Wirz's at Andersonville—seeing that he too did nothing more nor less than carry out policy?

CHIPMAN   You compare me to him?

BAKER   (*Starting for the door*)   You know in your heart that you condemn him only for carrying out the orders of his superior. (*Pausing near* CHIPMAN) You have as much as said so. But this Court will have no part of that argument. And what then do you do but withdraw it? You obey, as Wirz obeyed.

CHIPMAN   You compare me to him?

BAKER   Oh, of course, you're governed by purer motives. After all, you're on the edge of a brilliant career. You'll walk out of this case the envy of every struggling young lawyer in the country; the successful prosecutor of the one war criminal to be hanged out of this war. Yes, your future's assured . . . if you don't jeopardize it. Shall the government's own counsel at this time preach disobedience to orders? How does it feel to be an instrument of policy, nothing more?

CHIPMAN   Goddamn you—

BAKER   Get as angry as you wish—that's the truth of it. Good afternoon, gentlemen.

    (BAKER *and* SCHADE *exit*)

HOSMER Don't you see what he's trying to do? Provoke you into playing the idealist here?

CHIPMAN (*Moving restlessly*) I see—

HOSMER It would suit him perfectly to lead you down that path—

CHIPMAN I know—

HOSMER —to turn things so it's you arguing with the government—

CHIPMAN All right! (CHIPMAN *brings himself under control as he moves slowly to the doors and closes them before speaking*) I shout at you—I shout at Davidson—only a boy—a sick boy . . . (*He is silent for a long moment*) Where do we stand after days of those witnesses we've put on—those sick, broken survivors of that place? We haven't really proved conspiracy and we haven't proved criminal acts. And yet I know that behind Wirz's screams of innocence and persecution—behind that stance of the honorable wounded soldier who was only obeying orders, he hides something dark that must be smoked out—(*Breaking off, frustrated*) I ask you: What kind of case do we bring in here?

HOSMER If you want a better one, close with Gray. (*As* CHIPMAN *looks knowingly at him*) Eyewitness evidence that Wirz murdered—

CHIPMAN (*Withering*) Eyewitness evidence—

HOSMER   Let the Court decide—

CHIPMAN   You've heard Gray—do you believe him?

HOSMER   Let the Court decide—! (HOSMER *watches* CHIPMAN *move restlessly*) If you put him on you will finish strong. Gray furnishes the name of the murdered man; name and regiment. Good God, what difference does it make in the end, Chipman? Wirz is doomed anyway.

CHIPMAN   And the kind of case we bring in doesn't matter, does it?

HOSMER   Not—really.

CHIPMAN (*Flaring*)   But if there's a moral issue here—I mean if we feel that Wirz should have disobeyed—and if we evade that issue—if we're afraid to raise it—how are we actually any better than that creature was at Andersonville? Are we all Wirz under the skin? Feeding where we're kept alive? At a trough?

HOSMER   So Baker *has* reached you!

CHIPMAN (*With hard amusement*)   Do you think that? Or is it that he raises an issue which has been in this case from the beginning—and which we haven't wanted to face?

HOSMER   We don't *need* to face it. I'll say it again—Wirz is doomed no matter how our case looks. But you can make it hard for yourself if you turn it the wrong way. You're a soldier, you know how the Army has to function, if it is to function at all. It has ways of dealing with irregulars. Are you thinking of a Washington career or will you be satisfied with a law practice in some county seat in Iowa? (*Studying* CHIPMAN) Chipman, you seem to *want* to go a hard way.

CHIPMAN (*Sardonic; mimicking*) I *want to go a hard way.* This blood-spattered country—bleaching skulls in the woods —the dead of my own Iowa Second, names you wouldn't know—did any of us *want* to go a hard way? But we did—we did! As if we had any choice . . . as if I have any choice here. (*Pausing*) I asked for this case feeling *hard* against them— hating them enough to want to flog them through Wirz. (*At a pitch*) Do you think I *want* to shed that hatred? Understanding what Baker wants to do—to lock me in a quarrel with the government—I still can't go around that issue. I hate that damned Southern cause—and still I can't go around what Baker says. I'm partisan to my bones—and *still I can't go around it.* (*After a pause—in a lower voice*) I'd like to believe I'm more of a man than Wirz was; that, had I been in his place, I would have disobeyed if that was all that was left me to do to save those men . . . Yes, that's what sticks me . . . Am I more of a man than he was? (*Groping*) Either . . . either I press the Court to consider the issue of Wirz's moral responsibility to disobey or—I'm no better in my mind than he was! I can't go around *that.*

HOSMER And just how do you plan to go around raising the moral issue?

CHIPMAN I don't know—(*Reaching for something*) Let Baker put Wirz on the stand.

73

HOSMER Which he won't do . . .

CHIPMAN I know that. I know . . .

HOSMER Put on Gray. You don't have to like him . . . Just put him on. Nail down your case with a clear statement of murder—and you will have your man . . . even if it's not in *your* way— The government has a point to make, too, you know: it struggles to pull together a divided country. Isn't that a worthy, an important thing? At least as important as the purity of your soul? (HOSMER *waits, but* CHIPMAN *turns away.* HOSMER *goes to the door*) You stay?

CHIPMAN A moment . . . There are larger issues than a man's own convictions, aren't there?

HOSMER (*Tiredly*) Sometimes. (*A pause; and then, almost fiercely*) You make me feel old.
> (*He exits.* CHIPMAN *paces slowly; and, finally, without seeming to realize it, sits down in the witness chair, turning his head to look back toward the Andersonville map. Then, as he grasps that he sits in the chair, he brings his hands down to grip the arms of the chair, as if to say, "Here I am, too!"*)

The Curtain Falls

74

ACT TWO

Scene: the following morning.

At rise: the court personnel, lawyers and reporters stand about, chatting, waiting for the session to begin. The LIEUTEN- ANT *enters.*

LIEUTENANT   Attention!
  (*The* JUDGES *enter*)

WALLACE   At ease. (*The* JUDGES *and the others take their positions*) This Court is now in session. What is the pleasure of the Judge Advocate?

CHIPMAN (*Standing*)   If it please the Court . . . on the specification that the defendant committed murder by his own hand, we call Sergeant James S. Gray.

LIEUTENANT (*Calling out into the corridor*)   Sergeant James S. Gray.
  (*During the following exchange,* GRAY *waits at the door. He is a strong, tough-looking soldier—a type to bet on as the sole survivor of some desperate situation. He is dressed sharp, down to shiny cavalry boots*)

BAKER (*Seated*)   If the Court please, we do not see that name listed here.

CHIPMAN (*Moving to* WALLACE's *table, his voice noncommittal*) Sergeant Gray was not listed since it was uncertain that his

77

release from duty could be arranged in time. He is attached to General Thomas' headquarters at Nashville.
(WALLACE *glances inquiringly at* BAKER)

BAKER   No objection.

WALLACE   The witness may be sworn in.
(GRAY *enters, salutes smartly, is sworn and takes the stand*)

CHIPMAN (*The tone is flat*)   Sergeant Gray, what is your regiment?

GRAY   Seventh Illinois Cavalry, Company B, sir.

CHIPMAN   And how long have you been in the service?

GRAY   In my last term, two years and one month.

CHIPMAN   How long were you at Andersonville prison, Sergeant?

GRAY   I was taken to Andersonville on the tenth of June, 1864, and remained there until November.

CHIPMAN   Do you know anything about the defendant, Wirz, having shot a prisoner of war there at any time?
(WIRZ *tries to come to his feet;* BAKER *restrains him*)

GRAY (*His manner is calm and easy*)   He shot a young fellow named William Stewart, a private belonging to the Ninth Minnesota Infantry.

CHIPMAN   State the circumstances.

78

GRAY Stewart and I went out of the stockade with a dead body—

CHIPMAN Explain how you could get out.

GRAY The regulations were that whenever a man died, prisoners could be detailed to take the body out past the gate to the deadhouse.

CHIPMAN Continue, sir.

GRAY Well, sir, I had begged for the chance to move that dead body and I was picked with Stewart to take it out. We went up to the gate with the dead man and they passed us out with a guard. It was my determination—I don't know whether it was Stewart's or not—to try to make an escape again. We went toward the deadhouse, not to put the body into the deadhouse because in that house they were piled like cordwood full up and the line of dead bodies extended out from it about fifty yards. Wirz then came riding up and dismounted and asked us what we were doing out there. Stewart replied that we had brought out a dead body to place in the deadhouse. Wirz said it was a lie, that we were trying to make our escape. Stewart said it was not so. We came for purpose stated. Wirz said if you say that again I'll blow your brains out. Stewart repeated what he said before. Wirz then struck him down and stamped him and then drew his revolver and shot him—

CHIPMAN (*Pointing to* WIRZ) Is that the man?

GRAY Yes.
(WIRZ, *in a spasm of energy, leans forward, facing* GRAY)

79

WIRZ   Look close, Sergeant—make sure! I give you the chance to take back that lie before the great God judges you!

GRAY (*Cool and indifferent*)   You knocked him down and shot him dead—

CHIPMAN   That will be all.

BAKER   I ask for a moment to confer with the defendant. We have no preparation for this witness. (WALLACE *signals affirmatively*. BAKER *crosses to* WIRZ) Quick, who is Gray?

WIRZ   It's no use—

BAKER   Who is Gray?

WIRZ   I don't know.

BAKER   What about Stewart?

WIRZ   There was no William Stewart.

BAKER   Are you sure?

WIRZ   Yes—yes. I'm sure.

BAKER (*Turning toward* GRAY. *Restlessly searching*)   Sergeant, will you describe once more this so-called Stewart's death?

GRAY   Captain Wirz rode up and asked us by what authority we were out there. Stewart spoke up and said that we were out there by proper authority—

BAKER (*His manner sharper; openly skeptical*) So Captain Wirz knocked him down and shot him simply because he said he was out there by proper authority?

GRAY Whether he shot Stewart because he said that to him or because he was a Yankee, I don't know. I don't know why Wirz shot him. I leave that to himself. But that was all Stewart said to him.

BAKER There were some guards about when this so-called murder occurred, were there not?

GRAY I recall some.

BAKER Did you speak to them after Stewart was killed?

GRAY I never spoke to Johnny Reb if I didn't have to.

BAKER How well did you know Stewart?

GRAY (*Shrugging*) We were in the same prison squad.

BAKER And under what circumstance did he oblige you with his name and regiment?

GRAY I don't recollect exactly.

BAKER Describe this William Stewart.

GRAY All looked alike there. Thinned out and not to be recognized by their own mothers—

BAKER (*Circling* GRAY) So you cannot describe him. You talked to him and you know his name and regiment but you cannot describe this man. Did he hide his face while he talked to you? (*As* GRAY *is about to speak*) I know—thinned out and not to be recognized by their own mothers. Can you refer to any third person who could identify this William Stewart?

GRAY No.

BAKER No! What does that answer mean? There were ninety men in that prison squad with you and Stewart. Then other men—at least one—must have known he was from the Ninth Minnesota—and could identify him.

GRAY Counsel, he happened to mention his name and regiment to me—

BAKER (*Through his teeth*) However, fortunately for the prosecution which until now has lacked for a clear criminal instance, it has dredged you up as the single witness to the murder of a man having at least a name—(*Very hard*) Sergeant, do you believe in an afterlife and that man's sins, including the sin of lying, will there be punished?

GRAY I believe there is such a thing as punishment after death—

BAKER Have you ever been arrested for a criminal offense?

GRAY No, sir.

BAKER I gather you like Army life, seeing that you have re-enlisted.

GRAY   I would say that.

BAKER   After all, the Army feeds you, keeps you comfortable, and judging by your sergeant's stripes, you are considered by your superiors to be a good soldier, one who knows what he is supposed to do without it being explained to him in so many words.

GRAY   A man gets to know what is expected of him.

BAKER   And if you felt—even if you weren't told—what was expected of you, you would carry it out, wouldn't you?

GRAY   Certainly.

BAKER   And if you felt—even if you weren't told—what the Army's real concern was in some situation and if you understood that to mean that you were supposed to lie—

WALLACE   Finish your question along that line, Mr. Baker, and you will be in contempt—

BAKER   Withdrawn. Sergeant, what did you do before entering the Army?

GRAY   Farmed some; ran dogs.

BAKER   Ran dogs—?

GRAY   In hunting and so forth.

BAKER   Where did you do that work?

GRAY   In Illinois, Indiana, Virginia, and—

BAKER   Virginia . . . (*In a sudden intuition*) For what purpose did you run your dog pack in Virginia? Was it by any chance to bring back runaway slaves?

GRAY   Yes, sir.

BAKER   I take it it was more profitable to track down runaway slaves in Virginia than to hunt deer in Indiana.

GRAY   Yes, sir. Being as the nigra was valuable property that had to be brought back alive.

BAKER   Tell me, Sergeant. Did that valuable property ever make human sounds when you caught it and beg you to let it find freedom?

GRAY   I don't remember.

BAKER   Human feelings must be put aside sometimes, mustn't they? (GRAY *doesn't answer*) And the truth must be put aside sometimes, too. (GRAY *doesn't answer*) And when you said you saw Wirz kill a man named Stewart at Andersonville, you were lying, weren't you?

GRAY   I saw that happen as I have described it.

BAKER   That will be all.

CHIPMAN   (*Coming forward; furious*)   Sergeant Gray! *Were* you lying when you said you saw Wirz kill a man named Stewart?

84

GRAY   I saw that happen as I have described it.

CHIPMAN   Sergeant, I ask you again, did you see Wirz kill a man named Stewart or did you hear about something like that?

GRAY   I saw that happen as I have described it—*sir!*

CHIPMAN   . . . That will be all!

WALLACE   (*With distaste*)   The witness will step down. (GRAY *salutes and exits*) Has the Judge Advocate concluded his case?

CHIPMAN (*Crosses to table, sits, and after a sullen silence*)   Yes, sir.

WALLACE   Is the defense ready?

BAKER (*Rises; moves to face the Court*)   Yes, sir. If the Court please, since the defense regards the instance of murder alleged against the defendant as the single charge worth refuting—

WALLACE   The Court is not interested in your judgment of the charges—

BAKER (*Finishing*)   —we shall waive our entire list of witnesses and will in their place put on the stand one witness.

WALLACE   One witness?
        (WIRZ *stirs restlessly and turns to* BAKER *as if to speak*)

BAKER   Questioning will take no more than a few minutes and will constitute the entire defense case.

WALLACE   Who is the witness?

BAKER   He is in the room—Dr. Ford, the physician in charge at the Old Capitol jail, where the defendant has been lodged since the trial began.
   (WIRZ *mutters a protest to* BAKER, *who quiets him*)

WALLACE   Let Dr. Ford take the stand.
   (FORD *steps forward and is sworn*)

BAKER   Dr. Ford, have you, during some time past, been in the habit of seeing the defendant?

FORD   Since June, I believe, ever since his imprisonment he has been under my care when sick.

BAKER   Have you during that time examined his right arm and have you examined him today?

FORD   Yes, sir.

BAKER   What do you find to be the condition of his right arm?

FORD   It is swollen and inflamed; ulcerated in three places; and it has the appearance of having been broken.

BAKER   The fingers of his right hand?

FORD   Two fingers, the little finger and the next are slightly contracted. The contraction is due to an injury to the nerve leading down to the fingers.

BAKER   Have you examined the defendant's left shoulder?

86

FORD   Yes, sir. A portion of it is dead. There is a very large scar on the left shoulder and a portion of the deltoid muscle is entirely gone—I suppose from his war wound. It has been carried away, only the front part of the muscle remaining.

BAKER   How does that influence the strength of the arm?

FORD   (*Illustrating*)   He might be able to strike out with fore-arm from the elbow but he could not elevate the whole arm.

BAKER   And as to the right arm? Would he be capable with that arm of pushing or knocking a man down?

FORD   I should think him incapable of doing so with either arm, without doing himself great injury.

BAKER   Would he have been capable of using with force any heavy or light instrument—would he have been capable of pulling the trigger—let alone suffering the recoil of—a heavy revolver?

FORD   No—not likely.

BAKER   And as to his condition a year ago, in 1864?

FORD   I have spoken with Dr. Bates, who was at Andersonville and who examined Wirz there at the defendant's request, and he confirms my opinion that this condition was no better in 1864 than it is now.

BAKER   Then he could not have knocked down this so-called William Stewart—

FORD   I don't see how—

BAKER   He could not have pulled the trigger—

FORD   As I have said—

BAKER   He could not have killed him. The defense rests! Thank you!

WALLACE (*Harsh and strained*)   Will the Judge Advocate cross-examine?
>   (CHIPMAN *moves forward impetuously—stops*)

CHIPMAN (*Harsh*)   Dr. Ford has testified to Mr. Wirz's physical condition as he saw it and we are not here to dispute the medical findings . . . No cross-examination, but . . .
>   (CHIPMAN's *voice dies away, but he remains standing, inwardly, silently fighting*)

WALLACE (*Waiting, and then—*)   Thank you, Dr. Ford.

WIRZ (*To* BAKER; *a loud whisper*)   What is it? Is it all finished? But I have not had the chance—

WALLACE   We will convene the day after tomorrow to hear government and defense summations.

CHIPMAN (*In a burst*)   If the Court please, we ask for a continuance—!

WALLACE   Continuance?

CHIPMAN —until tomorrow morning. The Judge Advocate would like to determine if there is something pertinent to this trial—

WALLACE (*Sharp*) Does the Judge Advocate wish to bring forward new evidence?

CHIPMAN Possibly.

BAKER The defense will welcome new evidence—particularly on the charge of violent murder attributed to a man who cannot raise his arms.

WALLACE (*Gavel; he waits for a moment*) Unless the government contemplates other witnesses we must consider the presentation of evidence finished—
    (WIRZ *reacts with a choked sound of protest*)

CHIPMAN (*Glancing rapidly at* WIRZ; *his manner terribly strained; speaking in bursts of thought*) We do not feel that the situation at Andersonville has been thoroughly explored —that is why we ask the continuance—we feel there is more to be discovered—more to be said about what took place there—

WIRZ I agree—yes! For once I agree with the Judge Advocate!
    (WALLACE *raps*)

CHIPMAN (*Whirling to face* WIRZ) Does the defendant desire to take the stand in his own behalf?

WIRZ What?

BAKER What is that? . . . No, the defendant will not take the stand.

CHIPMAN (*Looking straight at* WIRZ, *speaking with desperate speed*) Of course he is not legally bound to do so, but it seems to the Judge Advocate that he might wish to make his position clearer than anyone else can possibly do for him—

BAKER (*Rising*) What is the Judge Advocate trying to do—?

WIRZ (*Leans toward* CHIPMAN) If I might wish *what? What*—?

BAKER (*Going on*) He addresses defendant over the head of counsel.

WIRZ (*Overlapping*) But what is it the Judge Advocate is saying—I would like to know what is meant—*that I might make my position clearer*—?

WALLACE (*The gavel rapping*) You cannot speak unless you take the stand, Mr. Wirz. The Judge Advocate is asking if you wish to take the stand. You have a right to do so, but cannot be compelled to do so. You have that right, though we suggest you listen to counsel.
(BAKER *and* SCHADE *stand over* WIRZ)

BAKER Are you out of your mind?

SCHADE I don't understand what's come over you!

WIRZ This legal game has been played back and forth and I am to die without a word to say for myself! I must explain—

90

BAKER   *Listen.* The evidence they've offered is tainted from start to finish. And they know it! Let them bring in their verdict of guilty. But it must then go to the President, who may pardon as he values the reputation of the government. That's your single chance—

WIRZ   And I say no chance. No chance—

SCHADE   Wirz, listen to Baker—

BAKER   You will not take the stand—

WIRZ   (*Standing up*)   I was a man like other men and I wish to show that!

BAKER   You'll face Chipman alone. You will be alone—

SCHADE   (*Overlaps*)   Do you understand? Alone!!

WIRZ   Yes, alone, as I have been alone—and neither you nor anyone here has been concerned for me as a *man*. And now— (*His manner is feverish. He crosses to face* CHIPMAN *and the Court*) I might wish to speak—since the Judge Advocate wishes me to take the stand—

WALLACE   I don't understand you, Mr. Wirz. You may or may not take the stand as *you* wish. It has nothing to do with what the Judge Advocate wishes.

WIRZ   And I am saying that I might do that. Since I have been slandered here I might do that. I don't understand what is the difficulty—(*Revealing a deep need, in spite of a tone of mockery. Moving to face the* JUDGES *at close range; glancing toward*

91

CHIPMAN) So the Judge Advocate wants me to take the stand—

WALLACE   The Judge Advocate can not influence you to do that. He is not your counsel.

WIRZ   No, no, of course he is not. He is my worst enemy. Oh, I know that. He wishes to destroy me. (*He looks steadily at* CHIPMAN *and* CHIPMAN *in turn looks back at him. There is something private between them now*) Take the stand, on my own behalf, eh, Colonel?

CHIPMAN   On your own behalf.

BAKER (*Grimly*)   Are you dispensing with counsel, Captain Wirz?

CHIPMAN (*Speaking with cool desperate calculation*)   Mr. Wirz, if you take the stand, you will speak for yourself. And after that—let me warn you—I will try to search you out to the bottom of your soul.

WIRZ   Hah! You think you can do that?

CHIPMAN   I can try—

WALLACE (*Gavel*)   Will the defendant say whether or not he wishes to take the stand!

WIRZ   General! (*Moving to* BAKER) Hah—do you hear that? My worst enemy—what does he say? He will search me out, to the bottom of my soul!

BAKER   You think Chipman is here to save you?

WIRZ   I am to die—I must take the stand! I have been made a monster in the eyes of my children. I die with that mark on me if I do not speak up! And I will not have it that way—I will give them my words so they can say their father was a man like other men. Do you understand me? (BAKER *looks at* WIRZ *searchingly.* WIRZ's *tone is strange*) You will examine— and then I will fight him.

BAKER   And if you take the stand . . . how will I keep you from saying more than you should?

WIRZ   But you see, Baker, I must fight him . . . (BAKER *stares hard at* WIRZ) I must . . . fight him.
          (BAKER *shrugs finally, his expression tired and a little sad. He turns to face the Court*)

BAKER   (*Slow*)   The defendant will take the stand in his own behalf.

WALLACE   He understands that he is not required to do so?

BAKER   The defendant understands and wishes to do so.

WALLACE   You may take the stand, Mr. Wirz.
          (WIRZ *is sworn and takes the stand*)

BAKER   (*His effort is plainly to be brief and to limit* WIRZ's *answers*)   Captain Wirz, you are a naturalized citizen of the United States, is that correct?

WIRZ   Yes, sir.

BAKER   When and where were you born?

WIRZ   I was born in Zurich, Switzerland, in the year 1822.

BAKER   What year did you arrive in the United States?

WIRZ   In 1849.

BAKER   Describe briefly your activities prior to the outbreak of the war.

WIRZ   I worked at first in the mills in Lawrence, Massachusetts, and, not doing well there, moved with my family to various parts of the United States. I lived in Louisiana for a time and resided in Louisville, Kentucky, when the war broke out.

BAKER   State your war record prior to your appointment as superintendent of the Andersonville prison camp.

WIRZ   I enlisted in the service of the Confederacy as a private and was soon commissioned as a lieutenant, having had previous military training abroad. After being wounded at the battle of Seven Pines I was offered that assignment of superintendent, by General Winder.

BAKER   Over what period of time did you serve in that assignment?

WIRZ   From January, 1864, until February, 1865.

BAKER   Were you at any time given special or secret instructions as to how you were to run that camp?

WIRZ   No, sir!

BAKER   I refer specifically to instructions for the care of the prisoners.

WIRZ   No, sir—no special instructions beyond the prescribed regulations for the care of prisoners of war, and any statement to the contrary—

BAKER   Captain Wirz, were the food supplies at first furnished you sufficient for the prisoners?

WIRZ   Yes, sir, at first I was given ample supplies to furnish for each and every enemy prisoner a ration which was the same ration issued to Confederate soldiers as is the custom. It included bacon and fresh baked bread daily. If not bacon, it was beef and those men did not starve, but later it became—

BAKER   Captain Wirz, state the circumstances under which that situation changed.

WIRZ   It began to change for the worse around March when we began to receive prisoners by the thousands but not sufficiently an increase in the ration. So I naturally had to cut down more and more that ration and I wrote to General Winder about that—

BAKER   When did you write that letter?

WIRZ   Sometime in May, 1864.

BAKER   (*Holding up letter*)   I have here a letter written by Captain Wirz to General Winder, dated May 19, 1864.
      (SCHADE *takes the letter to* WALLACE)

SCHADE   Presented to the Court.

WALLACE   (*After glancing at it*)   It may be entered in the record.

95

SCHADE (*Giving the letter to the* CLERK)   Letter of May 19, 1864, offered for the defense.

CLERK   Exhibit nine, for the defense.

BAKER   Captain Wirz, tell us about that letter.

WIRZ   Yes, sir. I wrote to General Winder about the lack of food and requested additional supplies.

BAKER   Now, Captain, did General Winder reply to that letter?

WIRZ   He did so in person on one of his visits to the camp. He said we were taking care of the prisoners just as well as the enemy took care of *our* men in *their* hands. He said he had reports that our men were not well treated, particularly at a camp at Elmira, New York, where they were dying like flies. He was in a temper and he made it clear *that* closed the subject, and as an inferior officer I felt I could not pursue the matter further. However, I did what was in my power to do there—as about those drummer boys—

BAKER   We will get to that in a moment. Tell the Court now the origin of the deadline.

WIRZ   Yes, as to that deadline. Well—in that conversation I said to General Winder that the prisoners were getting desperate because of the lack of food and the guards consequently nervous, fearing a rush on the walls, and there was bound to be trouble. I asked for more guards there to quiet the prisoners down with a show of strength. But he said men could not be spared. But still—it was my responsibility they should not escape, don't you see, so I suggested that inner line, and General Winder approved that line. But that did not mean I did not consider those prisoners, as I started to say before about those drummer boys—

BAKER (*Curtly*)   Very well. Tell the Court about those drummer boys.

WIRZ   Yes, sir. There were sixty or seventy boys in that camp, drummer boys, little bits of boys and I felt bad that these boys, no more than children, should suffer there, having children of my own. So I asked them if they would take an oath not to try to escape and they did and they were put on parole outside the walls and lived outside the camp. I assigned them to pick blackberries to provide additional food for the camp, but that did not work. Being boys, they ate what they picked themselves— And that was not all I did there—

BAKER (*Trying to control* WIRZ)   Captain Wirz. Tell us about Father Whelan—

WIRZ   Yes. I gave permission for all priests and ministers to enter that camp and Father Whelan, of the Roman Catholic Church, came several times bringing fresh bread there. He was allowed to bring that in and he distributed it to all the prisoners, black and white. All religious people of any denomination were permitted to enter to give comfort to the prisoners—all. I believe that religion is—that religion—

BAKER   Now, Captain, tell us about the women who tried to bring food into the camp.

WIRZ   Yes, yes— General Winder at first graciously consented to let that food in, but when those women were about to do that he received some bad war news, some report that Sheridan was burning farmhouses and crops in the Shenandoah Valley and he then flew into a rage and said that food couldn't be brought in and being an inferior there I could hardly override his orders. That is how it was. In general that place was entirely on my head—

BAKER   Did you try to get relieved—

WIRZ   (*Picking up in intensity as he goes on*)   I have not finished! I was saying that place was entirely on my head and I had there the responsibility to keep order and keep those men from escaping and they kept trying and it was difficult to keep order there since the men kept trying. Naturally they had that right to try and I had my duty which was to prevent them.

BAKER   But you did try to get relieved of that assignment, did you not?

WIRZ   Yes, sir, I tried to do that. I wrote to General Winder, asking to be assigned to another post, but he informed me he could not relieve me. And, simply—I had there to stay and so it kept on being on my head.

BAKER   I have here a letter written by defendant to General Winder, dated May 26, 1864, in which defendant requests that he be relieved of his post at Andersonville.

SCHADE   (*Takes the letter to* WALLACE)   Submitted for the defense.

98

WALLACE (*Glances at it*)   It may be entered.

SCHADE (*Takes the letter to the* CLERK)   Letter of May 26th, 1864, offered for the defense.

CLERK   Exhibit ten for the defense.

BAKER   Captain Wirz, did you strike down and kill a man called William Stewart?

WIRZ (*Shouting*)   There was no William Stewart and that is a lie—(WALLACE *raps the gavel.* WIRZ *repeats sullenly*) There was no William Stewart.

BAKER   Did you, at any time, shoot down or kill a prisoner of war?

WIRZ   No, sir; I never did that. I could not physically do that.

BAKER   Captain Wirz, when you were arrested at the conclusion of hostilities, were you making any attempt to escape?

WIRZ   No, sir; I saw no reason to do that. I was with my family outside the stockade and, having heard of the general pardon, was on my way back to Louisville when a major of General Wilson's forces entered to tell me I was under arrest. I was taken away and held prisoner. I soon understood the awful charge against me—and that my fate was to hang—!
(BAKER *abruptly tries to close off the examination*)

BAKER   That will be all, thank you.

WIRZ (*Shouting*)   Am I not to be asked my conception of my duty?

BAKER   Thank you, Captain Wirz.

WIRZ   I wish to explain how I understand the military rules!

BAKER   Very well. Explain your understanding of the military code.

WIRZ (*With bite and growing bitterness*)   That one does as he is ordered. That he keeps his feelings to himself. That he does not play the heroic game which some people who are not in his position think he could play. That he obeys. That he does not concern himself with the policies of his superiors—but obeys. That he does his assigned job and obeys. That when the order to charge is given—he obeys. That when ordered to keep prisoners—he obeys. And if in so doing he must die, then he dies.

BAKER   Your witness, Colonel.

CHIPMAN (*He is still for a moment*)   You have explained your sense of duty clearly, Mr. Wirz. When the officer is ordered to keep prisoners he obeys.

WIRZ   Yes, sir.

CHIPMAN   Meaning that he must keep the prisoners from escaping?

WIRZ   That is one of the things—yes.

Albert Dekker, George Scott, and Herbert Berghof,
as BAKER, CHIPMAN, and WIRZ

CHIPMAN   Meaning that he must keep them alive—?

WIRZ   As much as it is within his power.

CHIPMAN   Which did you regard as more important? To keep them from escaping or to keep them alive?

WIRZ   According to the customs of war, to keep them alive as it was within my power *and* to prevent them from escaping.

CHIPMAN   One duty neither more nor less important in your mind?

WIRZ   Both equal—

CHIPMAN   You say you never at any time killed a prisoner of war?

WIRZ   (*Raising his arms slightly*)   It has been demonstrated that I could not—

CHIPMAN   I ask *you,* sir, directly—did you or did you not—?

WIRZ   I never did that. No, sir.

CHIPMAN   In that letter of May 19, 1864, in which you tell General Winder of your increasing duties at Andersonville I note that you also ask him to consider a promotion in rank for you from captain to major. What were you concerned with when you wrote that letter? The overcrowding or your promotion?

WIRZ   It was nothing wrong in the same letter to request that promotion—

CHIPMAN And in your letter requesting a transfer from Andersonville you make a point of your illness as the reason—

WIRZ To make it indirect, otherwise General Winder might not have liked that transfer request.

CHIPMAN But you were in fact seeking medical attention when you wrote that letter, weren't you?

WIRZ I had in mind at the same time to get away from that assignment.

CHIPMAN You say that what occurred at Andersonville was beyond your power to avert?

WIRZ Yes, sir.

CHIPMAN In the course of performing your duties you inspected the stockade—at times I imagine from the wall where the sentries stood. You could look down into that—how would you describe it, may I ask?

WIRZ It has been described—

CHIPMAN As a sort of hell—?

WIRZ Oh, indescribable, sir. Indescribable. I suppose you remember, Colonel, hearing me say that I could not bear the sight of those young boy prisoners in there, sixty to seventy of them, and sent them out to pick blackberries—

CHIPMAN That is in your favor—

WIRZ   Thank you—

CHIPMAN   It is interesting that you keep referring to that act—
as if there is so much else you dare not remember—

WIRZ   You twist things, sir— I let Father Whelan bring bread—

CHIPMAN   You went to your duties from your home every
morning?

WIRZ   Yes, sir.

CHIPMAN   And I take it you were a normal father and husband,
concerned to raise your children properly and teaching them
the common virtues—?

WIRZ   Particularly in a religious way—yes.

CHIPMAN   And you saw nothing strange in leaving your family
and your grace at meals to go to your job of overseeing the
dying of those men?

BAKER   Objection.

CHIPMAN   Withdrawn. You have said that keeping those men
alive was of equal importance in your mind with the need to
keep them from escaping?

WIRZ   Yes, sir.

CHIPMAN   The food was wormy and rotten. Did you think of
sending out foragers to commandeer supplies from Georgia
farmers?

WIRZ It would have been illegal—

CHIPMAN You could have signed vouchers—

WIRZ I was not authorized—

CHIPMAN Payable by the Confederacy—

WIRZ Not authorized, sir—

CHIPMAN Sent out squads of prisoners to collect firewood—

WIRZ They would escape—

CHIPMAN Under guard—

WIRZ There were not enough guards—

CHIPMAN Enlarged the stockade—

WIRZ The size was prescribed—

CHIPMAN Let those prisoners among whom were carpenters, masons, and mechanics of all sorts, build the shelters which would have kept them alive—?

WIRZ As I have already said—not authorized—

CHIPMAN But those measures would have saved lives—

WIRZ I don't know how many!!—

CHIPMAN (*Flaring*) We will say only one!— Would say that one, single human life is precious, Mr. Wirz?

WIRZ   I do not follow—it would have been illegal for me to do the things you say—

CHIPMAN   But morally right, Mr. Wirz?

BAKER   Objection.

WALLACE   We do not see how the Judge Advocate's questioning connects with the charge of conspiracy.

CHIPMAN   (*Grimly*)   Will the Court allow me to explore that issue one step further before deciding the connection cannot be made?

WALLACE   (*With equal grimness*)   You may explore it—one step further.

CHIPMAN   Mr. Wirz, you are a religious man?

WIRZ   As I have testified—I know how important religion is, and I allowed all ministers—

CHIPMAN   Then, sir, professing religion as you do, would you agree that moral considerations, the promptings of conscience, are primary for all men?

WIRZ   Of course I do! I observe that ideal like most men—when —I—can!

CHIPMAN   When you can. Then you could not observe moral considerations at Andersonville?

WIRZ   That situation was General Winder's responsibility—not mine.

CHIPMAN (*Rising, moving closer to* WIRZ) You regarded that situation as General Winder's responsibility because he was your military superior?

WIRZ Yes—

CHIPMAN And how far did you deem his authority over you to extend?

WIRZ To all circumstances, considering that was a military-war situation.

CHIPMAN To all circumstances. Are you certain of that?

WIRZ I am absolutely certain!

CHIPMAN And had he, in that military-war situation, given you a direct order to slaughter one of your own children without giving you an explanation, would you have done that?

WIRZ That is ridiculous—

CHIPMAN Would you have done that?

WIRZ It is ridiculous—I do not answer—!

CHIPMAN Would you have done that?

WIRZ No—!

CHIPMAN Why not?

WIRZ It would be an insane order—!

CHIPMAN   Yes. Insane. Or inhuman. Or immoral. And a man therefore in his heart does indeed make some inner judgment as to the orders he obeys.

WALLACE (*Gavel*)   The Judge Advocate will hold. The Court has stated more than once, it is not disposed to consider the moral issue relating to soldierly conduct. It has indicated to the Judge Advocate that we are on extremely delicate ground at any time that we enter into the circumstances under which officers may disobey their military superiors. However, the Judge Advocate apparently feels he must enter that area. He will now advance some legal basis for that line of questioning or withdraw it.

CHIPMAN   If it please the Court—we will endeavor to connect this line—

WALLACE   The Judge Advocate must in advance furnish a legal basis—

CHIPMAN   The Judge Advocate respectfully urges—

WALLACE (*Gavel*)   The Court must hear some basis for permitting this line of inquiry.

CHIPMAN (*Desperately; demanding*)   If it please the Court, military courts—judging war crimes—are governed by both the criminal code and by the broader, more general code of universal international law. In most cases that come before them, they will judge specific acts in which the nature and degree of offense is determinable without great difficulty. But, on rare occasions, cases occur demanding from a court a more searching inquiry. Should the Court allow such broad inquiry it becomes more than the court of record in a particular case; it becomes a supreme tribunal—willing to peer into the very heart of human conduct. The Judge Advocate urges that the Court does not in advance limit or narrowly define the basis for questioning. Should the Court insist on such a basis, then we are through with the witness.

WALLACE   Does the Judge Advocate offer the Court alternatives?

CHIPMAN   We did not mean to imply that—

WALLACE   The Court is flattered to think it may take on the mantle of a supreme tribunal— However, it is still a military court.

CHIPMAN   If it please the Court—

WALLACE   No, Colonel, I'm not through. The Court grants it may be philosophically true that men have the human right to judge the commands of their military superiors, but in practice one does so at his peril.

CHIPMAN (*Slowly*)   At his peril, yes, sir.

WALLACE (*His tone is deadly*)   We would want that the peril of that line of questioning be understood most clearly. We have a question for the Judge Advocate that he may or may not answer—he is not, of course, on trial here. The question is: What is it an honest man fights for when he takes up arms for his country? Is it the state or the moral principle inherent in that state? And if the state and the principle are not one, is he bound not to fight for that state and indeed to fight against it? The Judge Advocate need not answer, for we will make the question more particular. If, at the outbreak of the war, the government of the so-called Confederacy had stood on the moral principle of freedom for the black man, and the government of the United States had stood for slavery, would a man have been bound, on moral grounds, to follow the dictates of conscience—even if it had led him to the point of taking up arms against the government of the United States?

CHIPMAN (*Anguished*)   It is inconceivable to me—

WALLACE   That is not the question—

CHIPMAN   That situation could not possibly occur—

WALLACE   That is not the question—

CHIPMAN (*Bursting*)   He would have been bound to follow the dictates of his conscience.

WALLACE   Even to the point of taking up arms against the government of the United States?

CHIPMAN (*After a pause; slow*)   Yes.

WALLACE (*With deliberateness*)   The Colonel understands, of course, that a man must be prepared to pay the penalties involved in violating the—let us say—the code of the group to which he belongs. In other societies that has meant death. In our society it can mean merely deprivation of status—the contempt of his fellows—exile in the midst of his countrymen. I take it the Colonel understands my meaning?

CHIPMAN   He understands what the Court is saying.

WALLACE   And he still feels that he must enter that dangerous area?

CHIPMAN (*Now he is pleading; no longer hard*)   General, I do not enter that area of my own free will. I enter because I have been forced to it by the nature of this case. (*Moving to the map*) We have lately emerged from a terrible and bloody war and that war has spawned a most sinister and curious crime. Men in the thousands—fourteen thousand men—have been sent to their death—not by bullets on the battlefield, but in a subtle, furtive, hidden manner. We have in the course of this trial examined as it were the outward appearance of hell—its walls, deadline, swamp, dogs, its terrible heat and freezing cold. But we have not gotten to the heart of it. We are now faced with the necessity of exploring further into—let us say it again—hell. (*At last* CHIPMAN's *underlying humanity comes through*) I put it to this Court that we owe to those fourteen thousand who died there—to those who mourn them—something so true as to put us head and shoulders above politics, above sectionalism, above the bitterness in our own hearts. I admit to entering this room with that bitterness in myself—I admit to the mood of vengeance. I would now wish to go beyond that if I can. As we say—life is precious—as we cling to our humanity by our fingernails in this world—by our fingernails—let us have a human victory in this room.

WALLACE (*After a pause*)   The Court is not unmoved. (*The pause is long as the* JUDGES *confer,* WALLACE *sitting still in the midst of them, disturbed and considering*) The Judge Advocate considers as primary to the presentation of his case the moral issue of disobedience to a superior officer?

CHIPMAN (*Strained*)   Yes, sir.
   (*Again* WALLACE's *pause is long; and then, almost angrily—*)

WALLACE   The Judge Advocate may continue—

BAKER (*Losing control of himself for the first time; incredulous*) The Judge Advocate may continue? Defense counsel is amazed that the Court does not now recognize there is no legal case here. To attempt to connect normal obedience to orders with willful conspiracy is impossible and no fine-sounding statement about universal law or supreme tribunal can bridge the unbridgeable. The Court knows the Judge Advocate cannot possibly make that connection. The Court knows that! And yet the Court allows the Judge Advocate to proceed when it should forthwith dismiss the defendant—

WALLACE   Is counsel ordering the Court to do that?

BAKER   No, but he submits there is no legal case here.

WALLACE   The Judge Advocate may continue—(*Sharply, as* CHIPMAN *takes a step toward* WIRZ) bearing in mind that the Court may conclude at any time that it feels there is nothing more to be gained from this line of questioning.

CHIPMAN (*Crosses slowly to* WIRZ; *tired*)   Mr. Wirz, we have said that a man does make some inner judgment as to the orders he obeys. That implies that if those orders offend his humanity deeply enough he may disobey them. The authority of General Winder over you was not absolute. And so the question is, why did you obey?

WIRZ (*Looking about him rapidly*) Am I required to answer? . . . I did not think of my assignment at Andersonville in that way . . . I do not understand what happens here . . . I thought only in the normal way to obey him, since he was my military superior—

CHIPMAN But not your *moral* superior, Mr. Wirz. No man has authority over the soul of another. As we are men we own our own souls and as we own them we are equal as *men*—the general, the private, the professor, the hod carrier. *We are equal as men, sir.* And every man alive as he is a man knows that—as you in your heart knew that—

WIRZ But that is not—

CHIPMAN And as that situation had become a grossly immoral situation, and as General Winder was not your moral superior, you did not have to obey him. So the question remains, *why did you obey?*
      (WIRZ *glances toward* WALLACE)

WALLACE The Court will hear the answer.

WIRZ (*Incredulously*) I will say it clearly. I would have been most certainly court-martialed. And if my superiors wished, considering it was a time of war, and that the war had come to a desperate, bitter stage in which the word "traitor" could be sounded in a moment—I might have been executed—

CHIPMAN It might at least have been for a reason. You might have saved fourteen thousand lives—were you afraid?

WIRZ I? A soldier? Afraid?

CHIPMAN (*Standing over* WIRZ) The question then still is— *Why did you obey?*

WIRZ As I have explained. What heroic thing do you demand I should have done at Andersonville? I—an ordinary man like most men?

CHIPMAN Mr. Wirz, we who are born into the human race are elected to an extraordinary role in the scheme of things. We are endowed with reason and therefore with personal responsibility for our acts. A man may give to officials over him many things. But not what is called his soul, sir—not his immortal soul. And the question therefore still is—*Why did you obey?*

WIRZ Why? As I have said. As I say for the last time—it was to me a military situation.

CHIPMAN But that was not a military situation, Mr. Wirz. Those helpless, unarmed men were no longer the enemy, whatever Winder said. Here was no longer a question of North and South; no longer a question of war; only a question of human beings. Chandler saw that. Those Southern women who brought food for those starving men—they saw that. Where was your conscience then?

WIRZ Where!!??

CHIPMAN In General Winder's pocket with his keys, his tobacco and his money. And worth no more than any of those things—

WIRZ You speak high, Colonel—high! Ask them in this room if they can say in their hearts they would have done different if they had been in my place—ask them (*In fury and contempt*) You are all the victors here and you make up a morality for the losers!

CHIPMAN Yes! The victor makes the morality since the loser cannot.

WIRZ And I spit on that morality! I spit on it! And I say—ask them in this room if they would have done different—ask them—

CHIPMAN And if they could not, then we must shudder for the world we live in—to think what may happen when one man owns the conscience of many men. For the prospect before us is then a world of Andersonvilles—of jailers concerned only to execute the commands of their masters. And freed of his conscience—fearing only the authority to which he had surrendered his soul—*might the jailer not commit murder then?*

WIRZ I did not commit murder!

CHIPMAN (*Circling*) You did not kill William Stewart?

WIRZ There was no William Stewart—

CHIPMAN (*Fiercely*) You were never in a fury with those men —a fury great enough to overcome the weakness of your arms?

WIRZ It is as the doctors say—

114

CHIPMAN (*Very close to* WIRZ)   To whom do you dare say that? You and I have both been on the battlefield. We've seen men holding their bowels in their hands and with their legs broken, still moving forward. You raised your arms—

WIRZ   No—!

CHIPMAN   Yes! You were in a fury when you rode out to hunt down those men with that dog pack and when you caught them you raised those two dead arms—

WIRZ   No—!

CHIPMAN (*Toward a crescendo*)   Then how did you rein that hard-mouthed horse you rode to the left—and how to the right—and how bring his head down when he reared—if not with those two—dead—arms?
   (*On the last phrase* CHIPMAN, *his face contorted, grabs* WIRZ *by the upper arms. As he does so,* BAKER *and* WALLACE *start, as if to speak, but* CHIPMAN *lets go as quickly as he had taken hold, horror in his face at his own act*)

WIRZ   Possibly!— I raise my arms sometimes! Yes!—but I did not kill any William Stewart because there was no William Stewart, so help me God.
   (CHIPMAN *stares at his hands. Both men are now near exhaustion*)

CHIPMAN   We will leave Mr. Stewart aside—but you had to obey orders which you knew were killing men, didn't you?

WIRZ   I had to obey—

CHIPMAN   Even though you knew that to obey was to kill those men—and to disobey was to save them?

WIRZ   (*Making a curiously helpless gesture*)   Even though—Simply—*I could not disobey.* I did my duty as I saw it. I have made that clear. But you badger me. Which however way I explain it, it will not do for you—and you badger me—you badger me! I have made it clear that I had to keep order there. To keep the record monthly of the number of prisoners including those escaping—to report that to General Winder and the War Department—and you badger me. It has been made clear—and *you will not let go.* To prevent them from escaping—to report in writing the attempted escapes—that was my responsibility. Isn't that clear? Even though I had not enough men, that did not excuse me, though I found that job overwhelming—isn't that clear? And you badger me! It *was* overwhelming and I had to find ways and means to block those escape attempts—that was my duty. It was solely on my head. So it went, I preventing, they trying, I preventing, they trying. And no move to stop them completely successful. Nothing, nothing could stop them. And that responsibility solely mine. The deadline—that did not prevent them. Cannon mounted on the wall—that did not prevent them. They kept trying. Tunneling under the walls. Digging, burrowing, burrowing— In the night, burrowing. Crushed from the weight of the wall timbers when they made the mistake to burrow directly under those logs. And the others continuing. Continuing. Tracked down by the dogs and trying again . . . and I having to anticipate . . . finding their tunnels . . . learning their tricks. They trying, I preventing. They trying, I preventing. They bribing the guards with greenbacks . . . blacking their faces to pass as niggers to bring the dead bodies out of the stockade . . . and I charged to block those moves. But nothing prevents them to try . . . that burrowing. At night. I'm awake. I don't need to see them to know what they are doing. Burrowing. In the night. Digging, digging, in that hopeless effort to escape—digging, crawling—like rats—

CHIPMAN   And rats may die and one may have no compunction about rats—

WIRZ   Yes—(*Catching himself*) I meant rats, so to speak— You are playing a cheap lawyer's trick on me—

CHIPMAN   Very well, a cheap lawyer's trick—so they were not rats to you—*but they were no longer men to you.* In your mind you canceled them out as men and you made them less than men, and then they might die and one did not have to suffer over that, did he? (*Almost gently*) Why did you try to commit suicide in your cell? (WIRZ *is silent*) Is it because you feel nothing? (*Silence*) Is it because you have no human feeling left and cannot endure yourself feeling nothing? (*Silence. In sad contempt*) You speak too much of your children . . . ! Is it because you have already—in your mind—asked them— Should I have done my duty or should I have given a man a drink of water?—and you heard their answer? (WIRZ *starts;* CHIPMAN'S *tone is one of confirmation, very soft*) Yes . . . you wish to die. (*Silence.* WIRZ *stares off. And now* CHIPMAN'S *tone is one of pained, exhausted inquiry—no longer hunting*) I ask you for the last time, Mr. Wirz. Why—and it was not fear of court-martial or dismissal or any external thing—why—*inside* yourself—couldn't you disobey?

WIRZ (*In a low, relieved exhalation*)   Simply—I—could not. I did not have that feeling in myself to be able to. I did not have that feeling of strength to do that. I—could—not—disobey.

CHIPMAN (*Moving with slow, dragging, exhausted steps to the government table*)   The government rests.

The Lights Dim Out Quickly

Scene Two

A week later.
As the lights come on, WIRZ *stands erect, and* WALLACE *is well into the reading of the verdict.*

WALLACE . . . and on the charge that the prisoner did with others conspire to destroy the lives of soldiers in the military service of the United States in violation of the laws and customs of war— Guilty. And on the various specifications that he aided and abetted murder and did commit murder— Guilty. And the Court do therefore sentence him, the said Henry Wirz, to be hanged by the neck till he be dead, at such time and place as the President of the United States may direct, two-thirds of the members of the Court concurring therein. The business of this military court being now terminated, we declare the Court dissolved.
  (*The gavel raps once.* WIRZ *is led out. The* JUDGES *go out quickly. Then there is a general exit.* BAKER, *with* SCHADE *at his shoulder, crosses to* CHIPMAN)

BAKER I'll say this for you, Colonel. At least you fought on your own terms.

CHIPMAN I asked for Wirz's guilt—not his death.

BAKER But he dies anyway. His life for the Union dead. No matter that you so stubbornly fought to purify the occasion— it was a political verdict—whatever you said.

CHIPMAN   I charged him for what he is. Perhaps, deep down, the Court did, too.

BAKER   Perhaps. It was a worthy effort though it hasn't anything to do with the real world. Men will go on as they are, most of them, subject to fears—and so, subject to powers and authorities. And how are we to change *that* slavery? When it's of man's very nature?

CHIPMAN   Is it?

BAKER   Isn't it?

CHIPMAN   I don't know. We try.

BAKER   (*Ironically*)   We redecorate the beast in all sorts of political coats, hoping that we change him, but is he to be changed?

CHIPMAN   We try. We try.
> (BAKER *goes out, followed by* SCHADE. HOSMER *looks at* CHIPMAN's *grave face, pats him gently on the shoulder and goes out. For a moment longer* CHIPMAN *looks at the map—the hieroglyphic which bespeaks a more engulfing disaster than he grasped in the beginning. He goes out. The lights dim, leaving only a light on the Andersonville map, which fades slowly as*

The Curtain Falls